THE BIBLE IN
WORLD
EVANGELISM

THE BIBLE

in World Evangelism

A. M. CHIRGWIN

A study sponsored by the
United Bible Societies

FRIENDSHIP PRESS   NEW YORK

First published in England by
Student Christian Movement Press, Ltd.
March 1954

Lithographed in the United States of America

CONTENTS

PART THREE

CONCLUSIONS

FOREWORD

IT is as an individual rather than as President of the United Bible Societies that I express my delight in Dr. Chirgwin's book. I have felt in reading it that the sources of the past open up and become fruitful again, and I believe that those who read it will be inspired to live up to the adventure of the Bible, the book of today and tomorrow.

There is a touch of imagination in this book. The glimpses which it gives of ancient times and distant places widen our horizon and at the same time make us feel an urgent drive to use the Bible in future evangelism. The background of the Bible and the story of the way in which the Holy Spirit has used it are presented in such a fashion as to give us joy and confidence and courage. The reader can find this out for himself and thus discover a new and joyful responsibility. Or if he does not want any new responsibility he can read the book for sheer delight.

EIVIND BERGGRAV
BISHOP

Oslo

PREFACE

THE UNITED BIBLE SOCIETIES invited me, early in 1951, to undertake a study of 'the place of the Bible in evangelism' as some contribution to the preparation for the Evanston Assembly of the World Council of Churches. That study has been my main task for the last two or three years, and some of the most important conclusions to which I have been led, together with some of the relevant material on which the conclusions have been based, are contained in this book. The collection of the data has entailed a good deal of reading, correspondence, discussion and travel. I am deeply indebted to a host of helpers in many parts of the world, and in particular to my colleague Olivier Béguin, the General Secretary of the United Bible Societies, and to my honoured friend Bishop Berggrav who read the whole manuscript and then put me still further in his debt by writing a brief foreword.

A. M. CHIRGWIN

Geneva,
Christmas, 1953

Part One

THE PLACE OF
THE BIBLE IN EVANGELISM
IN THE HISTORY OF
THE CHURCH

IN THIS SECTION the aim will be to show the relation of the Bible to evangelism through the long centuries of the Church's history. A full treatment of the subject is out of the question within the compass of this enquiry. All that is possible is to pick out the more vital and formative epochs and try to discover what place the Bible had in evangelism at those times. The periods that have been chosen, or rather that have suggested themselves are, firstly the Early Church, secondly the great renewal eras such as the Reformation, the Puritan and Pietist movements and the Evangelical Revival, and thirdly, our own time.

I

IN THE EARLY CHURCH

AT THE TIME when the Church was born no one expected that it would produce a book which would come to occupy a central place in its life. The Founder of the Faith neither wrote anything Himself, nor encouraged His disciples to write. He sent them out to preach and teach, and to bear witness of that which they had seen and heard, and all the evidence goes to show that they did it by word of mouth. Yet in spite of that a book came into existence and came to be an indispensable element in the Church's life. How did this happen and what were the influences that brought it about?

One of the influences was that the young Church realised the need to get the gospel down in writing before the original eye-witnesses passed from the scene, and before the message itself was forgotten or corrupted. Thus Mark is said to have written down the substance of Peter's conversation and public addresses, and Luke to have put into book-form what he heard Paul say, and what he gathered from other sources. The motive was to get a permanent record before it was too late.

Another influence was an urge to pass on the Christian message to others so that they too might know the gospel story. 'What thou seest write in a book and send it to the seven Churches which are in Asia.' The aim was to hand on the Good News. The motive was evangelistic. Paul's Epistles, for example, had the same evangelistic purpose as his addresses, namely 'to preach Christ and him crucified'. The writer of the fourth Gospel says quite explicitly that 'these things are written that ye might believe that Jesus is the Christ, the Son of God, and that believing ye might have life in his name'. The New Testament writers were not just writing history; they were writing for a verdict.

A third influence that helped to bring the New Testament into existence was the frequent journeyings of many of the earliest Christians. They seemed to be always on the move. Peter went to Caesarea and Joppa; Philip went to Samaria and the South Country; Paul and Barnabas went to Antioch and from there started on their great missionary journeys that took one or both of them over much of Western Asia and Southern Europe; Priscilla and Aquila went from Rome to Corinth; Timothy from Rome to Ephesus; Luke from Troas to Athens; Apollos from Alexandria to Rome. They criss-crossed the world of their time. 'If we were to mark on the map the routes of all their journeys which are known to us, the lines would make a labyrinth'.[1] This constant movement of the early Christians and the consequent winning of converts in place after place was an important influence in bringing the New Testament into being. These new converts and communities could not always have an Apostle in their midst. Yet they needed someone or something to keep them on the right lines. Some substitute for an eye-witness had to be found and the written accounts were the substitute. As Luke told his friend Theophilus, his purpose in writing was 'that thou mightest know the certainty of those things wherein thou hast been instructed'. The new converts were the ones who most of all needed accurate written records. How else could they be sure of their facts? And how else could they hand on the word to others? The New Testament documents, as Canon Herklots says, were the propagandist

[1] H. G. G. Herklots, *A Fresh Approach to the New Testament*, p. 14.

literature of a widespread and successful missionary movement.[1]

A fourth influence was the pressing need of the young Churches in places like Galatia and Macedonia, Greece and Rome, and elsewhere. Some needed counsel, others reproof, yet others much fuller instruction than they had received. The Epistles, which comprise half the New Testament, were written to meet precisely these needs, and they came from the hands of those who could speak with authority. Some of them were meant for more than one group of Christians and were in the nature of circular letters. 'When this letter has been read to you', Paul writes at the end of his Epistle to the Colossians, 'arrange for it to be read in the Church of the Laodiceans also, and see that you read the letter that reaches you from Laodicea.'

A fifth influence arose from the fact that most of the earliest Christians, being Jews by birth, were accustomed to hear the Hebrew Scriptures read both in the synagogue and at home. Jesus, like every other Jewish child, was familiar with them from His earliest days. According to a recent writer, Jewish school children of that period 'received little parchment rolls, specially prepared for school purposes, containing passages which had to be learnt by heart.'[2] There was nothing unusual therefore in the fact that Timothy 'knew the Scriptures from childhood' or that the Beroeans 'searched the Scriptures daily'. The unusual element appeared when they began to use the new writings, such as the Gospels or the Epistles, side by side with the ancient and revered Hebrew Scriptures.

This new practice created a problem, for since a number of

[1] H. G. G. Herklots, *A Fresh Approach to the New Testament*, p. 13.

[2] P. Levertoff, "The Jewish Elementary School in the First Century A.D." in *The Teachers' Commentary*, p. 257.

writings, some old, some new, were coming to occupy a central place in the life of the young Church it was important that there should be agreement about which ones were to be regarded as suitable; in other words, about which books should be in the Bible and which should not. Some people, e.g. Marcion, wanted to omit the whole of the Old Testament and much of the New Testament as well. Others, for example Justin, argued that the Old and New Testaments formed a unity and could not be torn apart or treated separately without missing their meaning. Some people wanted this book included, others wanted that. It was obviously necessary for someone to make a decision on the matter. The decision was made not by any committee of scholars or Council of Bishops. It was made by the Church as a whole. Those books that were most often read and found most useful came to be regarded as canonical or worthy of a place in the Bible, while those that were not often used or were not found very illu-minating quietly dropped out. It was an effective method, though it took a good many years before a final canon or list of Scriptures was generally adopted. It was also an appropriate method, for the sacred writings had arisen out of the Church's life and been preserved by the Church's care, and it was therefore right and proper that the Church as a whole should say which books should be in the Bible and which should not.

Tertullian, who seems to have been something of a lawyer, or at least to have had a lawyer's mind, argued that since the Scriptures were God's gift to the Church, they belonged to it and were its property. On this basis, he built up his argu-ment and represented the Church as standing guard over its demesne, and asking, 'By what right, Marcion, are you cutting trees in my forest? How can you, Valentinus, under-take to change the course of my springs? Who authorises you,

Apelles, to displace my landmarks? By inheritance from the Apostles I possess the Scriptures and I alone.'[1]

Logical though this argument was, it did not convince everyone. Methodius, for example, declared that even though the Church might claim the exclusive ownership of the Scriptures, it was not free to interpret them in any way it might choose. Its interpretation must be in accordance with the mind or sense of Scripture as a whole. In other words, the Church must justify its interpretation at the bar of Scripture itself. So that though it was the guardian of the Scriptures, it could not treat them as it liked. They remained the final court of appeal and the measuring-rod of the Church's faith.

A book of sacred writings thus came into the possession of the young Church before it was two centuries old. This was a little surprising, for no one had ever set out to provide it with an authoritative book, or even argued that it ought to have one. But gradually, and without any human contriving, one came into existence. It consisted partly of the time-honoured Hebrew Scriptures and partly of new writings. These put together were what Jerome referred to as 'the Divine Library', on the ground that there were many books in one, and that Greek writers, using the plural form, called 'The Books' (*Biblia*). Popular usage, on the other hand, used the singular form, stressing their unity, and spoke of them as 'The Book'.

The place that the Bible came to have in the life of the Early Church is shown pretty clearly by the part it played in the great controversies and heresies that shook the Church's life. In the debates that took place there was constant appeal to the Scriptures. They were evidently well known to

[1] Tertullian, *De Praescriptione Haereticorum*, 30-40. Quoted in R. M. Grant, *The Bible in the Church*, p. 88.

Christian people generally and regarded as authoritative. Tertullian, for example, in his great controversy with Marcion, bases his argument entirely on Scripture. He takes it for granted that everyone recognises the authority of the Scriptures and possesses a copy with which he can verify his quotations and references. He and the other controversialists of the time never once suggest that the Bible is for scholars or clergy only. They regard it as everyman's book, and they assume that it is open to all. Tertullian maintains[1] that what the Scripture says it says to everyone and that every man can read it for himself. During the whole period of the Early Church, say, the first five centuries, there was never so much as a hint that the Bible was not open to everyone. The evidence is all in the opposite direction. 'From a child thou hast known the Scriptures' (II Tim. 3.15), Paul writes to Timothy; while he urges the Colossians to 'let the word of Christ dwell in you richly, teaching and admonishing one another in psalms and hymns and spiritual songs'. 'Let the Scriptures be in your hands', says Cyprian to his African flock. 'I cannot sufficiently urge you to devote yourself to the reading of the Bible', writes Jerome to the widow Demetrias. Clement and Tertullian both advise married couples to read the Bible together and to make it a feature of their family life. Origen speaks frequently about the desirability of reading it at home, and says that he himself as a boy was encouraged to learn passages by heart. He adds that he often perplexed his father with questions about what he heard and read. 'We have here', says Harnack, 'a glimpse into the home of an ordinary Christian citizen: the children daily hear the Scriptures read and learn passages of them by heart. A Bible was not only in the home, it was the principal

---

[1] Tertullian, *De Praescriptione Haereticorum*, 8-12, and A. Harnack, *Bible Readings in the Early Church*, p. 51.

text-book of education; the chief aim in the whole training of a child was that he should be taught to understand the Bible.'[1] A little later Chrysostom, in one of his sermons, developed the theme that the Bible is to the Christian what the tool is to the artisan. 'Every Christian', he says, 'should buy one and should never part with it.'[2] He urged a poor man who might feel that he could not afford a Bible to sell one of his tools to buy one. He excuses only the absolutely destitute and he urges them, by way of compensation, to pay particular attention to the Scripture readings in church.

Some of the poorer Christians, like Hilarion, copied out parts of the Bible for themselves. There is not much doubt that at that period the Bible was not only the Church's book, it was regarded as every Christian's book.

This emphasis on Bible reading was largely what helped to make the Christians a literate people. The Church urged them, in spite of their modest means, to buy and study the Scriptures. And it did so not because that would raise them in the educational scale, but because it was necessary that they should have direct access to the Word of God for themselves and be able 'to give a reason for the faith that was in them'. The motive was not the cultural or educational advantage of the members of the Church—any such advantage was a by-product—but the deepening of the spiritual life of the individual Christian and of the Church. Chrysostom is quite explicit on the point and his sermons show that he was constantly trying to plant the Bible in the home. He made a practice of announcing his Scripture lessons a week in advance so that the congregation might read them beforehand, and he also urged that after worship was over they should go home and read the lessons again 'with wife and children'.

[1] A. Harnack, *Bible Readings in the Early Church*, p. 75.

[2] Chrysostom, *Homily III on Lazarus*.

It was his firm conviction that if he could establish regular
Bible reading in the home he would thus lay a solid foundation for a truly Christian life.[1] It was this persistent pressure
that made the early Christians a surprisingly literate people
and the early Church a schoolmistress of the Graeco-Roman
world.

The centrality of the Bible in the life of the Early Church
seems from this brief sketch to be beyond question. What
remains to be investigated is its place in the Church's evangelistic and missionary activity. The available evidence seems
to show that from the first the Church regarded the Bible
not only as a necessary source of its life and faith but also as
an indispensable tool of its expansion.

There is abundant evidence of this in the New Testament.
In the Acts and the Epistles there are several accounts of the
way in which the Christian message was presented to non-
Christians. Some of those accounts are so vivid that we almost
feel, as Professor Foster says, that we are listening-in to the
first preachers as they harangued the crowds, to Peter on
the Day of Pentecost, to Stephen before his accusers, to Paul
on Mars Hill or in the court-room at Caesarea. What stands
out in all these accounts is the way in which the speakers
appeal to Scripture. They not only present their message in
biblical language, they also use the words of the Bible to
drive their message home.

There is also plenty of evidence in the life of the Early
Church. Justin, for example, in his 'First Apology', says that
in the Christian Church, as in the Jewish synagogue, sermons
were based upon Scripture. 'On the day called Sunday', he
writes, 'there is a meeting for all in one place', and he goes on
to say that the Gospels are read, or alternatively the Prophets,

[1] Chrysostom, *Homily III on Lazarus.*

as long as there is time, and when the reader has finished the
president gives an address based on what has been read.
It seems clear that the addresses of the early preachers were
based on the Scriptures and full of quotations from them.
Moreover, the reading of the Scriptures was regarded as
important for the spreading of the faith. Chrysostom says
that the readings were full and frequent, and he urged people
to make a habit of listening to them.

This appeal to the Scriptures seems natural enough when
Jews who were brought up on the Hebrew Scriptures were
being addressed, but it seems an odd thing to appeal to them
when the audience was made up of pagans. The Scriptures
meant nothing to them, and one would not expect them to
be moved by arguments based upon such documents. Odd
as it may appear, that is what was done. Aristides, one of the
earliest of the Apologists, writing not to Jews but to pagans,
urged them after reading his letter to turn to the Bible and
read it for themselves;[1] while Chrysostom argued that a man
could find in the Bible all that he needed to understand the
faith. It seems beyond dispute that the early Christian
preachers and writers constantly used the Scriptures as a
means of persuading non-Christians to accept the faith. The
Bible was the regular tool of their evangelism.

What is more, events proved the method right. The Bible
did in fact win converts. Its constant use by Christian preachers
and advocates led enquirers to turn to it and read it for themselves. This so often led to conversion that the view came to
be widely held that 'the regular way to become a convinced
Christian was to read the Holy Scriptures'.[2] It was by reading
the Bible that Justin, Tatian and Theophilus, according to
their own statements, became Christians. Justin's interests

[1] Aristides, *Apology*, 16.
[2] A. Harnack, *Bible Readings in the Early Church*, p. 42.

were, he tells us, wholly philosophic, and he attended the lectures of many of the best-known philosophers of the time. He studied under a Stoic, a Pythagorean, and a Platonist—in turn. But none of them satisfied him. At last an old man 'led him from Plato to the Prophets, from metaphysics to the Gospels'.[1] Hilary, Victorinus and Augustine were also among those whose conversion was due to the reading of the Bible. The story of Augustine's conversion never grows stale. By the age of thirty-three he had tasted every kind of amusement and distraction that the life of the time could offer, from serious study to unbridled lust, but the only result was a mood of self-loathing. In deep distress he flung himself under a tree in his garden in Milan and for hours lay in black despair, breaking out at last into the agonised cry, 'How long, O Lord, how long?' In response he heard a voice clearly saying '*Tolle, lege*' (Take, read). He jumped to his feet, snatched up his Bible, opened it and read: 'Put ye on the Lord Jesus Christ and make not provision for the flesh . . . to fulfil the lusts thereof.' 'No further did I read', he said, 'nor needed; for instantly at the end of this sentence a light, as it were of serenity, flooded into my heart and all the darkness of doubt vanished away.'[2]

It is not to be wondered at that the Church urged that the Bible should be open and available not only to Christians but also to non-Christians, for experience clearly showed that it was a missionary beyond compare.

This experience of the evangelistic value of the Bible led to the taking of a step which was to have results far beyond the wildest dreams of those who were first responsible for it. It led to the translation of the Scriptures which in its turn led to the opening of a new chapter in the cultural as well as the

[1] Foakes-Jackson, *History of the Christian Church*, p. 158.

[2] Augustine, *Confessions*, viii, 29.

religious life of whole peoples, in that it laid the foundations
of national literature in country after country that had no
literature of its own and possibly not even a written language.
This, however, was a by-product. It was not what the translators sought. What they aimed at was simply and solely the
spread of the gospel. Their motive was evangelistic. They
were eager to break through the barrier of language and set
the Scriptures free in new language areas. They certainly
took up the task with enthusiasm. By A.D. 200 they had
translated the Scriptures in part or in whole into Syriac, Latin
and Coptic, that is, into the principal languages of the east,
the west and the south. A couple of centuries later parts of
the Bible were also available in Ethiopic, Gothic, Armenian,
Georgian, and small portions in one or two other tongues.
It is a remarkable achievement and can only be explained as
the result of a deep evangelistic urge. The translators, moreover, were acting more wisely than they knew, for they were
preparing in advance for the fall of Rome. There is something
providential in the fact that before Rome was sacked some
part of the Bible was available in most of the main languages
of the time. Though Rome fell to the conqueror the Word
of God remained free.

From this same evangelistic urge another development
arose, namely the practice of reading the Scriptures aloud in
public or semi-public places.

Chrysostom says that these readings sometimes went on
for as long as two hours at a time. The aim, of course, was to
enable illiterate folk or those who had no Bible of their own
to hear the Word of God. The Church knew from experience that, given the chance, the Bible would win its own
way, and it took steps to make the Scriptures known to
Christians and non-Christians alike. It seems beyond question
that the Early Church regarded the Bible as a main tool of

its expansion and a foremost agent of its evangelistic advance.

The Christian Fathers were, of course, well aware of the dangers inherent in this policy. They knew that the interpretation of the Scriptures by individuals might lead to errors and heresies that would cause grave trouble in the Church. But they had no hesitation in running the risk. At no time did they oppose the wide, general use of the Bible, or attempt to reserve it and its interpretation to the officials of the Church.

Throughout the period of the Early Church the Bible was everyman's book. It was read at home as well as in Church; it was taught to the children and sections of it were learnt by heart; even poor people were urged to buy at least a Gospel and if necessary to sell in order to do so; above all, it was used as a means of presenting Christian truth to non-Christian neighbours. It was, in a word, the early Christian's *vade mecum* and remained in general use until the lay-folk began to grow tired of Bible-reading and to say that they were too busy with other things to give time to the Scriptures. In one of his sermons, Chrysostom takes them to task for this. 'The worst thing about it', he says, 'is that you believe that Bible-reading is purely a matter for monks. You say, I have to give my attention to public business; I carry on a trade; I must look after my wife and children and servants; in short, I am a man of the world; it is not my business to read the Bible; that is the business of people who have renounced the world and devote themselves to a lonely life upon the tops of the mountains'.[1] Chrysostom administered this public rebuke because he saw that there was a danger that Bible-reading might pass from the lay-folk to the clergy. What he feared actually came to pass. Bible-reading gradually ceased to be the practice of every Christian and became more and more the concern of the cloister. In fact the day was to come when the

[1] Chrysostom, *Homily III*.

laity were told that there were many reasons why they had better leave it to the clergy. In the centuries that followed no attempt was made to bring it back into the hands and homes of the people until the time of Waldo and Wycliffe. The Bible had by that time become so firmly embedded in the life of the monastery that it took the Reformation to restore it to the common people.

It must not be assumed from this that in the long period between the Early Church and the Reformation there was no interest in the Bible. Far from it. The Bible was far and away the most widely read book of the period. No one can dip even casually into the religious literature of the Middle Ages without being deeply impressed by the sheer mass of material that has to do with the Bible. There was copying and illuminating of Gospels and Psalters; there was translating of individual books or even of the whole Bible, as, for example, Methodius's notable achievement in the ninth century of translating the whole Bible into Slavonic; there was lecturing and teaching that had to do with the Scriptures; there were glosses and commentaries and postils without number. The time and toil that went into the writing and copying of these documents, many of which still survive, must have been prodigious. Some of them were master-copies meant for the monastery library. Some were workaday documents intended for the use of students. Others had comments in the margins or between the lines. Yet others were like paraphrases or running commentaries on the biblical text.

One scholar would publish his gloss on some part of the Scriptures; shortly afterwards another would put out his comments upon it; after that a third man would issue his gloss on both. The documents formed a kind of literary conversation carried on between the scholars of the time. They were, in fact, the medieval equivalent of the papers or proceedings of a present-day learned society. Scholars quoted and borrowed from one another; they glossed and re-glossed; they even tended to make a full-time activity of it. Anselm, we are told, set out to gloss the whole Bible,[1] though he never finished it. Others attempted almost equally ambitious tasks. Much of their output seems nowadays rather futile and artificial, but by the thirteenth century there were real gains to be recorded. There was such a copious biblical literature that a man could look up his text in a kind of concordance, find a list of variant readings and discover what the leading commentators had said about it. 'Glosses, dictionaries and other aids to study filled several shelves in any well-stocked library.'[2]

It is precisely at this point, however, that misgivings arise. In spite of the fact that the Bible was without question 'the most studied book of the Middle Ages', it never seemed to reach the people. It was confined to the cloisters and the clerics. Boniface's intimate knowledge of the Scriptures, for example, was gained during his years in the monastery, while Stephen Langton, one of the best-known biblical lecturers in the medieval period, said quite frankly that he regarded himself as teaching 'the prelates of the future'.[3] The laity were not invited or expected to share in this biblical activity, and the glosses and postils which were the stock in trade of the biblical scholars were completely remote from the life of the people.

This biblical activity was, moreover, largely artificial and allegorical. It had little or no relation to the biblical text. A scholar would take a passage of Scripture and interpret it according to his own presuppositions or those of his school without attempting to find what the original writer intended to say. Leading authorities like John Scotus Erigena in the

[1] B. Smalley, *The Study of the Bible in the Middle Ages*, p. 60.
[2] *Ibid.*, p. 366.   [3] *Ibid.*, p. 249.

tenth century or Bernard of Clairvaux in the twelfth 'took it for granted that the Bible was to be read allegorically, not literally'.[1] A good illustration of the prevailing fashion may be found in the writings of Hugo, the learned principal of the school of St. Victor in Paris. Commenting on the statement in Gen. 6.15 that the Ark was 50 cubits wide, he says that 'the width of 50 cubits signifies all believers, for 50 is made up of seven sevens, that is 49, a number that stands for the totality of believers, and one more, meaning Christ, who is the head of the Church and the consummation of our desires'.[2] It is easy to see that this kind of biblical activity did not so much interpret the Scriptures as obscure them.[3]

Another reason for the failure of the biblical activity of the Middle Ages to bear fruit was that the Church took fright and clamped down upon Scripture reading and study. Sects began to appear, and to make a practice of appealing to the Scriptures in support of their particular positions and also of showing how far the Church had departed from the teachings of the New Testament. Fearing that this practice might grow, the ecclesiastical authorities determined to put a stop to the reading of the Bible by the laity or at least to bring it under strict supervision. Thus Innocent III in the thirteenth century, insisted that 'since the Scriptures contained many things difficult to understand and liable to lead the ignorant and simple-minded astray, they should not be read except under the guidance of those competent to interpret them correctly'.[4] He also frowned upon unauthorised translations and after his day they were frequently proscribed and the faithful forbidden to have copies of them in their possession. A few years later, in 1229, the Council of Toulouse

[1] A. C. McGiffert, *A History of Christian Thought*, Vol. II, p. 170.
[2] *Ibid.*, p. 253.   [3] Stephen C. Neill, *The Christian Society*, p. 138.
[4] A. C. McGiffert, *ibid.*, p. 347.

made the ban complete, laying it down that 'no layman should be allowed to have any book of the Old Testament or of the New Testament, especially in translation, "unless perhaps the Psalter, a Breviary, or the Hours of the Virgin".'[1]

Beyond question there was plenty of biblical activity during the medieval period; but equally beyond question it did not reach the people. It took the Reformation to make the Bible once again the people's book.

[1] H. W. Hoare, *Our English Bible*, p. 100.

II

IN THE RENEWAL PERIODS
OF THE CHURCH'S LIFE

1. *The Reformation*

THE Reformation was not just the throwing off of the Roman yoke. It was a deeper movement with more sides to it than that. In part it was a protest against the abuses and corruptions of the medieval Church; in part it was an assertion of the new sense of nationhood against the dominance of Rome; in part it was a rediscovery of the Bible. And from the point of view of the present enquiry this last was probably the most important of all, for the rediscovery of the Bible was the chief source of the specifically religious element in the Reformation.

One of the features of the period was a widespread new interest in the Scriptures. It showed itself in many countries —Holland, England, Germany, Switzerland, France and Spain. New translations began to appear. For the first time, scholars began to push their enquiries back beyond the Vulgate in the hope of finding early Greek and Hebrew texts. There was a growing interest in the Scriptures, greater in fact than there had been for centuries. Did this new interest bring about the Reformation, or did the Reformation create the new interest? It is impossible to dogmatise, for evidence can be quoted on both sides. On the one hand there are plenty of facts to prove that the new interest in the Bible preceded the Reformation; on the other hand, it is beyond dispute that the Reformation gave the Bible back to the people. If there had been no rediscovery of the Bible, as far as one can tell, there would have been no Reformation (or it would have been a very different kind of Reformation); at

the same time, if there had been no Reformation the Bible
would not have reached the people as a whole. The truth
is that the affairs of the period were too closely interwoven
to disentangle them completely, or to say that this was cause
and that was effect. The facts seem to show that the rediscovery of the Bible and the Reformation grew up side by
side, acting and reacting on one another. First one made a
move and then the other followed suit. A glance at the dates
shows this happening. In 1516, Erasmus published his Greek
New Testament and the very next year Luther nailed his
thesis to the church door in Wittenberg. In 1522 Luther
translated the New Testament into German and a few years
later German princes and cities began to call themselves
'Protestant'. Again, in 1525, Tyndale translated the Bible
into English and in two years' time Reformation doctrines
were being openly advocated in Oxford and Cambridge.
Once more, in 1535, Olivétan translated the Bible into
French and a year later Calvin published his *Institutes* and
Geneva went Protestant. Every new step in biblical discovery
or translation seemed to be the occasion, if not the cause, of
another development in Protestantism. The biblical renewal
and the Reformation moved forward together, with the
biblical renewal generally taking the lead.

They also moved forward gradually. In both cases there
was a long period of preparation. In France the preparation
began as far back as Peter Waldo, in England as far back as
Wycliffe, and in Central Europe as far back as John Hus.
Waldo did not translate the Bible, but he had translations
made which his 'poor men of Lyons' carried into thousands
of villages and homes from Piedmont to the Pyrenees.
Wycliffe went further. He himself translated the Bible into
the speech of the common people and then sent it into every
part of the land. In some cases his 'poor preachers' carried

copies in the folds of their robes, in other cases they learnt large portions by heart and recited them wherever folk would listen. They taught men to prize above all things the right to read and study the Word of God for themselves. Hus, who was a professor in the University of Prague, was an acknowledged disciple of Wycliffe. 'I confess', he said, 'that members of this University and myself have possessed and read his works for 20 years and more.' There was much coming and going at that time between Oxford and Prague,[1] and Hus wholeheartedly adopted Wycliffe's views regarding the corruption of the Church, the authority of the Bible and the need for renewal. Years later, Luther, finding in the library at Erfurt a volume of Hus's sermons, said, 'When I read the title I was curious to know what doctrines he had propagated. On reading, I was astonished. I could not understand for what cause they had burnt so great a man, who explained the Scriptures with so much gravity and skill.'[2] All three, Waldo, Wycliffe and Hus, were pioneers in the rediscovery of the Bible and in the paving of the way for the Reformation.

In the following years, interest in the Bible steadily grew. It was mostly found amongst those who could read Latin, and edition after edition of the Vulgate appeared. But not amongst such people only, for vernacular translations also appeared. In fact, translations of the whole Bible were published in German, Italian, French, Danish, Dutch, Slavonic, Bohemian and Spanish before the end of the fifteenth century, that is to say, before the beginning of the Reformation.[3] These were of course translations of a translation, being made from the Latin Vulgate, as compared with those of the Reformers which were made from the original Hebrew and

[1] Hastings Rashdall, *Universities in the Middle Ages*, Vol. II, p. 232.
[2] H. B. Workman, *The Dawn of the Reformation*, Vol. II, p. 117.
[3] H. W. Hoare, *Our English Bible*, p. 119.

Greek. But whether the translations were made from the Vulgate or from the original tongues, there was a whole crop of them circulating in England and on the Continent before either Luther published his theses or England broke with Rome. The new interest in the Bible, so far at least as translations are concerned, certainly preceded the Reformation and probably helped to bring it about.

It is the special distinction of the Reformers that they put the Bible in the forefront of their movement. They declared that it was everyman's book, that it belonged not to the scholar or the priest, or to any section or group within the Church, but to every Christian everywhere. It must, they said, be available to everyman because it contains the offer of salvation that God has made to all men everywhere. 'Holy Scripture', says that typical Reformation document, the Thirty-nine Articles of the Church of England, 'contains all things necessary to salvation, so that whatsoever is not read therein, nor may be proved thereby, is not to be required of any man, that it should be an article of the Faith, or be thought requisite or necessary to salvation.' The Reformers held that God had spoken so fully and finally in the Bible that there was no need for anything more. Scripture, in their view, was not one of several pillars of the house of faith; it was the only one, or at least the only essential one. They dismissed the Roman claim that the tradition of the Church was the standard of faith on the ground that the claim had no scriptural warrant. That was the test they applied to everything. 'The Bible whole and alone' was their motto, taking up the cry with which the Waldensians had once made their valleys ring. For Luther, the Bible was the Word of God not because the Church said so, but because in its pages he came face to face with God. He knew, from that moment, that he needed no further assurance. God had met with him and spoken to him in the Bible and that was sufficient. For Calvin also the Bible contained all that a man needed to know to become a Christian. The Bible, he said, was the single and sufficient authority and was attested both by the answer of a man's own spirit and by Scripture itself.[1] Its proper place was in everyman's hands.

From this they argued that the Scriptures must necessarily be available in a language that everyone could understand. 'I totally dissent', wrote Erasmus in the 'Exhortation' to his New Testament, 'from those who are unwilling that the sacred Scriptures, translated into the vulgar tongue, should be read by the unlearned. I would wish even all women to read the Gospels and the Epistles of St. Paul. I wish they were translated into all languages, so that they might be understood, not only by Scots and Irishmen, but also by Turks and Saracens. I wish that the husbandman might sing parts of them as he follows the plough, that the weaver might hum them to the tune of his shuttle, that the traveller might beguile with their narration the weariness of his way.' Luther and Tyndale and Olivétan went even further. They not only wished that the Scriptures might be translated into the common tongue, they set themselves to do it.

The motive that actuated the Reformers was first and foremost evangelistic. They wanted everyone to have the chance to read the Bible because they believed profoundly in its converting power. Many of them had themselves experienced that power. Tyndale, for example, was brought to a new understanding of the Christian faith through reading the Bible for himself. Luther was set alight by the Epistles to the Romans and the Galatians. From the moment of these experiences both of them knew themselves called to make the Scriptures known to others. They realised that if God had

[1] Calvin, *Institutes*, I. vii, 5.

spoken to them in the Bible, they were in duty bound to give others the same chance to hear the divine word. Erasmus even advocated the sending of the gospel to the non-Christian world. In Asia and Africa 'there are', he wrote, 'barbarous and simple tribes which could easily be attracted to Christianity if we sent men among them to sow the good seed.'[1] Nothing happened as a result of this plea, though it was the logical conclusion of the Reformers' claim that every man should have the chance to meet God for himself in the Scriptures.

In our survey of this period two facts have emerged. One is the central importance given to the Bible by the Reformers themselves. The Reformation took different forms in different countries, due to national, personal and other circumstances, but on one point it never differed; never at any time or in any country did it fail to acknowledge the Bible as God's full and final word to man. The Reformation in Britain was a very different thing from the Reformation in Germany; similarly the Reformation in Switzerland followed a very different course from the Reformation in Sweden, but in every country the Bible was acknowledged as the record of God's revelation and the touchstone of faith. This centrality of the Bible gave the Reformation its vitality and marked it off from the medieval period.[2] The other fact is the importance attached to translating the Bible. The Reformers were as different from one another as men could be, yet they were alike in urging the translation of the Bible and in sharing in it. Nearly all the leading Reformers, however many other tasks crowded upon them, took a hand in Bible translation, and some of them made it their first priority. The reason was that they were convinced that the Bible contained all that was necessary for salvation and also that it

[1] G. Smith, *Short History of Christian Missions*, Chapter X.
[2] Stephen C. Neill, *The Christian Society*, p. 137.

was meant for all men. This was in point of fact one of their greatest contributions to the growth of the Church. In language after language they made the Scriptures intelligible to the common man.[1] Luther translated it into German, Tyndale into English, Olivétan into French, to name only three. It was not an accident that these three were at one and the same time Reformation leaders and Bible translators; it was the inevitable corollary of their view of the Bible, and between them they put it into the centre of Europe's life, where it became like leaven in the dough. In every country where it was given a chance it created something like a revolution.

2. The Puritan and Pietist Movements

We turn now to the Puritan and Pietist movements, as marking another of the renewal periods in the Church's life. The first thing to be said about them is that they had their roots in the Reformation and like it drew their sap from the Bible. In the countries where the two movements found their fullest expression, that is to say in Britain and Germany, the Bible brought about something like a revolution moulding their thought and salting their speech. In England the effect of the Bible upon its life during the Puritan period has never been better described than in J. R. Green's well-known words: 'No greater moral change ever passed over a nation than passed over England during the years which parted the middle of the reign of Elizabeth from the meeting of the Long Parliament. England became a people of a book, and that book was the Bible. . . . The whole temper of the nation felt the change. A new conception of life superseded the old. A new moral and religious impulse spread through every class.'[2] Similarly, in Germany the Bible, or at least

[1] Stephen C. Neill, The Christian Society, p. 160.

[2] J. R. Green, A History of the English People, pp. 460–2.

Luther's vigorous translation of it, became a potent influence in the national life and a landmark in German literature. It standardised the German tongue in much the same way as the Authorised Version standardised English.

To take the Puritan movement first. The Puritans took the Reformation seriously. They not only proclaimed its central truths, they put them into practice. They showed, for example, that the Reformation attitude to the Bible involved sending a man to find out for himself what the Bible had to say on personal and public affairs. This was not only a new and revolutionary notion, it had a tremendous effect on men's minds. It led them to discover that a man could sit by his own fireside with his Bible open before him, and could, by reading and prayer and by the guidance of God in his conscience, decipher its meaning for himself and his nation, and that he could do so without priest or squire or any other earthly person to help him. This was typical of the Puritans. They applied the Bible with a deadly earnestness to personal and national affairs. Did they, it may be asked, apply its message with equal vigour to the wider world?

It is often said that they were so absorbed in the fight for civil and religious liberty that they forgot about evangelism and missionary effort. While there is some truth in this, it does them much less than justice. They not only saw the missionary significance of the gospel, they responded to it. For instance, they granted charters for the planting of colonies which contained strong recommendations to undertake missionary activity. The royal charter of the colony of Virginia specifically stated that the purpose of the enterprise was 'to proclaim the Christian religion to such people as yet lived in darkness'; while the charter of the colony of Massachusetts, granted a few years later, urged the settlers 'to win the natives to the Kingdom of the only true God'.[1] More interesting still is the fact that in 1660 there was formed 'The Corporation for the Promoting of the Gospel among the Indians of New England', which was in all probability the first missionary society of the Protestant era. Even Cromwell may be cited in this connection. For he went down to Whitehall, Bible in hand, and induced Parliament for the first time in English history, to vote a considerable sum of money for missionary work overseas. It seems clear that for the Puritans in England the Bible and evangelism were not divorced, while in North America, as we shall see, they were closely linked.

When the Pilgrim Fathers and their successors migrated to North America they found themselves cheek-by-jowl with a non-Christian population. It was the first time that the Puritans came into close contact with non-Christians, and their reaction was unhesitating. They made the evangelisation of the Indians a real part of their new life. The difficulties of establishing friendly relations with them soon caused some of them to regard the Indians as 'Canaanites' whose extermination was a sheer necessity. Others persisted in their evangelistic purpose. Roger Williams, for example, the founder of Rhode Island Colony, learned their language in order to be able to preach to them in person. John Eliot, however, is the outstanding figure. He gave half a century of devoted service on their behalf and is rightly regarded as 'The Apostle of the Indians'. He was, in point of fact, the first missionary that America produced and one of the first of the Protestant era. It was the story of his work among the Indians that led Cromwell, as we have seen, to persuade Parliament to make a grant for missionary work abroad. Eliot had no sooner

[1] K. S. Latourette, *History of the Expansion of Christianity*, Vol. III, p. 44.

come in touch with the Indians than he realised that if he was to do any worth-while work amongst them he must have the Bible in their own language. In this he anticipated the almost universal experience of missionaries in later days. He accordingly set himself to translate the Bible into Mohican, and when he finished it, it was one of the first books to be printed on the American continent and 'the earliest example in history of the translation and printing of the entire Bible in a new language as a means of evangelisation'.[1] The fact to be noted is that as soon as the Puritans came in touch with the non-Christian world, their first act was to translate the Bible, and the reason for this was that they regarded the Bible as the best evangelistic tool at their disposal.

The name that is always linked with Eliot's is that of David Brainerd, another New England Puritan, who also poured out his life in the service of the Indians, and left a burning story that has been the inspiration of countless others. In these men the missionary passion of Puritanism burnt with an intensity that has rarely been surpassed. Roger Williams, John Eliot, David Brainerd, all soaked themselves in the Bible. They regarded it as the source of their missionary zeal and the essential tool of their missionary service.

Even though the Calvinists of Switzerland cannot properly be dealt with under the heading of 'Puritans', it is worth mentioning that a missionary venture was launched in Geneva with Calvin's active support as early as 1556, when a little expedition of eighteen men and women, sponsored also by the Huguenot Admiral Coligny, set out for Brazil. The venture was short-lived, but the fact that it was made serves to show that within a few years of Luther's death and while Calvin was still alive and before Elizabeth had come to

[1] Darlow & Moule, *Historical Catalogue of Printed Bibles*, Vol. II, p. 1093.

the throne of England, Protestantism was demonstrating its concern for the non-Christian world.[1]

The Pietist movement of the late seventeenth and early eighteenth centuries was in many respects the equivalent on the Continent of the Puritan movement in Britain and North America. Like Puritanism it had no organisation; it was a movement of the Spirit and was marked by a deep devotion to the Bible and a firm belief in its evangelistic power. Beginning in the Reformed Church in Holland it soon spread to the Lutheran Church in Germany, where it found congenial soil and put down its roots and grew. Its influence on the thought and life of Continental Christianity for a century and more was a feature of the time. Its main emphasis was laid upon group study of the Bible, the place of lay-folk in the Church and the promotion of overseas missions. Its influence was decisive in the case of the Moravians, and through them it reached to the Methodists and many others. Its chief glory, however, was that 'by its means the great Protestant missions were set on foot.'[2]

Pietism found a focus in Halle where a restless zeal for studying and circulating the Bible was combined with a burning passion for overseas missions.[3] The leader in both phases was A. H. Francke, the professor of oriental languages in the University. In his student days at Leipzig he and two others had launched a plan of Bible classes for students. The plan caught on, and Bible study grew to such proportions that the booksellers of the town could hardly keep pace with the demand for Greek New Testaments, while many of the

[1] G. Baez-Camargo, *The Earliest Protestant Missionary Venture in Latin America*, p. 4.

[2] R. Sohn, *Outlines of Church History*, p. 193.

[3] Stephen C. Neill, *The Christian Society*, p. 195.

students became so absorbed in it that they did hardly any other reading. Trouble with the authorities followed and eventually Francke was expelled from the University. He moved to Halle which soon became the headquarters of German Pietism. He restarted the Bible classes, opened a hostel for students and threw himself into the work of the Canstein House printing press which was producing Bibles and New Testaments by an ingenious method of printing rather like stereotyping, and selling the copies for a few pence each. The press had been started by Baron von Canstein in 1710, and he left it in his will to Professor Francke. Its aim was not to make profits but to print and distribute the Scriptures. It was rather like a Bible society born before its time. At any rate, before the British and Foreign Bible Society was founded Canstein House had printed over three million Bibles and New Testaments in various languages and dispersed them over Europe, America and even parts of Asia.[1]

In addition to directing the affairs of Canstein House, Francke devoted a good deal of time to his hostel for students with whom he shared his growing passion for overseas missions. Before long some of them began to dedicate themselves to missionary service, and in time a small but steady stream began to flow from Halle to the mission field. Halle, in fact, became 'the first nursery of missionaries outside the Roman communion since the Reformation'.[2] The first missionary appointments came in an unexpected way. King Frederick IV of Denmark surprised his friends, for his morals were known to be lax, by expressing concern for the spiritual welfare of his subjects in the Danish settlements in India. He ordered enquiries to be made for men

[1] William Canton, *History of the British and Foreign Bible Society*, Vol. I, p. 147.

[2] C. P. S. Clarke, *A Short History of the Christian Church*, p. 403.

suitable to be sent as chaplains. Finding none in Denmark, but hearing that there were some in Halle, he had them interviewed and two of them were duly commissioned for service in Tranquebar. They arrived in India in 1705, the first Protestant missionaries in that country. Faithful to the Halle tradition of devotion to the Bible one of them, Ziegenbalg by name, set himself to translate it, and in a dozen or so years he was able to report that most of the Bible was in the Tamil tongue and that a little band of converts had been won. Once more the Bible and evangelism went hand in hand.

It is significant that from the first Protestant missionaries, true to the Reformation principle of the Bible for the people, set themselves to translate the Scriptures into the vernacular. Long before John Eliot began his work among the Mohicans, the Jesuits had appeared on the scene, but they made no attempt to translate the Scriptures. Similarly in South India. 'The Roman missions had been at work in the Tamil country for 172 years before the arrival of the Protestants. In all that time they had not, as far as is known, translated into Tamil a single chapter of the Scriptures.'[1] This is one of the clearest differences between Roman and non-Roman missionary work.

Ziegenbalg was not the only Halle student to make missionary history. Amongst those who lived in the hostel for a time was young Count Zinzendorf, who, though hardly more than a boy, was already fired with a vision of the world-wide expansion of Christianity. A few years later he saw a chance to make his dream come true, when a number of refugees from Moravia, humble Bible-loving peasants, the spiritual descendants of John Hus, took refuge on his estate in Saxony. He made them welcome and under his leadership the Herrnhut estate became the centre of one of the most remarkable enterprises in missionary history.

[1] Stephen C. Neill, *The Christian Society*, p. 195.

The whole community dedicated itself to missionary work, and in two decades they had done more to spread the faith than the whole of Protestantism had done in two centuries.

It may be said, by way of summary, that Puritanism in Britain and Pietism on the Continent put the Reformation into practice. What the Reformation advocated they carried out. The Reformation made the Bible available in the common tongue. Puritanism and Pietism taught the people to read it, to meditate upon it and to apply its message to themselves and their times. Pietism even began to print and distribute it in large numbers. Both movements became aware of its missionary significance and set on foot pioneer missionary enterprises, one in India, the other in North America, not to mention the short-lived venture in Brazil.

3. *The Evangelical Revival and the Missionary Enterprise*

The Evangelical Revival and the missionary enterprise that grew out of it formed together one of the great renewal periods in the history of the Christian Church. Throughout most of the eighteenth century religion was formal and rationalist, and the Christian cause, especially in Britain, counted for very little in the common life. The people as a whole paid scant heed to the Church, while the bishops and clergy became a byword for worldliness and indifference. 'Several bishops never went near their dioceses. In many churches services were only held once a month by a visiting curate hired for the purpose by a non-resident rector.'[1] The outstanding exception was Bishop Butler who, when he was offered the Archbishopric of Canterbury, declined it on the ground that 'it was too late for him to try to support a falling Church'. It was the age of 'reason', and enthusiasm, especially religious enthusiasm, was regarded as the worst of follies.

[1] D. C. Somervell, *A Short History of Our Religion*, p. 252.

Yet it was religious enthusiasm in the form of the Evangelical Revival that was destined to stir the stagnant waters and to send the ripples to the ends of the earth.

Basically the Evangelical Revival was a return to the Bible, or at least it was accompanied by such a return, in much the same way as the Reformation was accompanied by a re-discovery of the Bible. In the years immediately before the Revival the Bible had not been suppressed; it had merely been neglected. It was a book that few read and fewer acted upon. The first indication of a change came when a little group of men in Oxford began to read together the Greek New Testament and Law's *Serious Call to a Devout and Holy Life*. Before long, the group broke up but the men themselves never looked back. In a few years' time some of them found themselves preaching to vast crowds, often in the open air. There was, moreover, a note of urgency in their preaching which men had not heard before. A new religious energy seemed to pulse through the veins of the people, expressing itself in developments as different as the rise of Methodism, the birth of the modern missionary enterprise, the abolition of the slave trade and the first stirrings of a social conscience. Lecky describes it as a 'new and vehement religious enthusiasm passing through the middle and lower classes'[1] and he traces it back to something that took place at an insignificant little meeting in the heart of the City of London on 24th May, 1738. The events of that day are described by John Wesley in his private journal. After mentioning his reading in the Bible in the morning and his hearing the Scriptures at a service at St. Paul's Cathedral in the afternoon, he continued, 'In the evening I went, very unwillingly, to a Society in Aldersgate Street where one was reading Luther's preface to the Epistle to the Romans. About a quarter before nine,

[1] W. E. H. Lecky, *England in the Eighteenth Century*, Vol. III, p. 146.

while he was describing the change that God works in the heart through faith in Christ, I felt my heart strangely warmed. I felt that I did trust in Christ, Christ alone, for salvation. And an assurance was given me that He had taken away my sins, even mine, and saved me from the law of sin and death.' That occurrence was not only the turning-point in Wesley's life but also a milestone in the history of the Church. According to Lecky it was even more. 'It is,' he writes, 'scarcely an exaggeration to say that the scene which took place at that humble meeting at Aldersgate Street forms an epoch in English history.'

As for Wesley, it sent him out into the highways and hedges and made him the greatest evangelist of his day. For fifty years he travelled up and down Britain, preaching everywhere. He averaged fifteen sermons a week and 5,000 miles on horseback a year. Here is a typical day as he recorded it in his journal: 'Preached at Gloucester at five in the morning to two or three thousand people; at eleven preached at Runwick to more than a thousand, and again in the early afternoon; then at Stanley a sermon two hours long to about three thousand; and finally a sermon at Ebley.'

At the heart of all this ceaseless evangelism was the Bible. It was its message that warmed Wesley's heart in the little room in Aldersgate Street. It was the Bible that linked him with Luther whose preface to Romans was being read. Luther and Wesley were brought together, because, as a recent writer has put it, they were both 'men of one book'.[1] There was what may be called a biblical succession linking Wesley through the Moravians, under whose auspices the meeting in Aldersgate Street was held, not only with Luther but also with Hus and Wycliffe. It was a remarkable chain and every link in it was concerned with the Bible.

[1] F. Hildebrandt, *From Luther to Wesley*, p. 151.

Wycliffe pioneered in Bible translation and John Hus acknowledged his debt to him. Hus in his turn planted the Bible in the heart of Bohemia, where the Church of the Brethren, as the Moravians were called, grew up. Later on a treatise by Hus made a deep impression on Luther's mind and still later a commentary by Luther, read at a Moravian meeting, set Wesley's heart alight and started the Evangelical Revival. Wycliffe, Hus, the Moravians, Luther and Wesley were all in the biblical succession, each name constituting a link in the chain.

The Evangelical Revival was not only rooted in the Bible, it gave the Bible a central place. Wesley's travelling preachers, for example, went through the land with the Bible in their pockets and the flame of evangelism in their hearts. No one can read their story without realising that the Bible was their constant companion and the invariable source of their evangelistic preaching. They soaked themselves in its language; they knew large parts of it by heart; their sermons were often little more than biblical passages strung together on the theme of God's plan for man's salvation. They familiarised the masses of the people with the words and message of the Bible as the parish clergy had not done for a century or more.

Nor was it only among the Methodists, who were mostly humble folk, that such things took place. Men of substance and culture, like those who formed the 'Clapham sect', were drawn into the company of the evangelicals. They read the Bible diligently themselves, and they also launched organisations to make it more widely known. They helped to start Sunday schools whose central aim was to teach the Bible; they encouraged the running of Bible classes and often conducted them themselves; above all they founded Societies for the printing and circulation of the Scriptures. The British and Foreign Bible Society was their most notable achievement, as it was also the clearest possible demonstration of the close connection between the Evangelical Revival and the Bible, in that those who founded it were evangelicals to a man.

The Evangelical Revival was thus in large measure a return to the Bible. It made the Bible the source of the preacher's message and the substance of the gospel he declared. It used the Bible as its main, if not its sole tool of evangelism. It placed the Bible in the home and built up around it the practice of family prayers. Above all, it founded Societies for the express purpose of making the Bible available to all men everywhere. There can be no question that at this great renewal period of the Church's life the Bible played a determinative part.

As we have seen, the Evangelical Revival was the source of many new beginnings. Amongst these none was destined to play a more important part in the world as a whole than the missionary enterprise. It transformed the face of Christendom and showed Christianity for the first time in generations as a dynamic religion, claiming the whole world for its Lord. It swept forward in breath-taking strides. Indeed, the hundred years following the Evangelical Revival have been called by Professor Latourette the 'great century' in view of the fact that it witnessed the greatest expansion of Christianity since the days of the Apostles.

But the modern missionary enterprise did not grow up alone. It grew up side by side with the Bible cause. They were associated at the start and they have kept together ever since. The fathers and founders of the two movements were convinced that they were necessary to one another, and they launched them on almost the same tide. A glance at the dates will make this clear.

In Britain the Baptist Missionary Society, the London Missionary Society, the Church Missionary Society and the

Methodist Missionary Society were born between 1792 and 1818, while the British and Foreign Bible Society came into being in 1804, right in the middle of that period. The Bible was at the heart of the newly-emerging missionary enterprise. Exactly the same thing is seen in North America, where four of the largest missionary societies—the American Board, the American Baptist, the Methodist and the Episcopal—were formed between the years 1810 to 1821, while the American Bible Society was founded in 1816, again right in the middle of the period. On the European continent in the 25 years between 1797 and 1822, the Netherlands Missionary Society and the Netherlands Bible Society, the Paris Missionary Society and the French Bible Society, the Danish Missionary Society and the Danish Bible Society were all formed. Never was there a period in which so many missionary societies and so many Bible societies came into being. It cannot be just chance that the formation of Bible societies is closely associated with the founding of missionary societies. The instances are too many and they are drawn from too many countries for them to be written off as mere coincidences. The only satisfactory explanation seems to be that the Bible, by the very nature of its message, leads to the formation of missionary societies, and missionary societies, needing Bible societies, help to bring them into being.

This close association may be seen again in the names of those who shared in the founding of the missionary and the Bible societies. To take Britain as an example, though the same is true of America, Germany and Switzerland, the same names appear again and again on both lists. To put the lists of the founders side by side and to note the number that occur in both is an impressive experience. The Treasurer of the London Missionary Society, for example, was also one of the founders of the Bible Society. So was the Treasurer of the Church Missionary Society. Deeply committed though they were to the promotion of missionary work, they felt they must also have a share in helping forward the printing and distribution of the Bible. The Secretary of the Church Missionary Society even went so far as to become one of the first secretaries of the Bible Society, and to hold both offices at the same time. Quite a number of those who took a leading part in starting one or other of the missionary societies were also active in getting the Bible societies established. They evidently thought it was not enough to start a missionary society; a Bible society also must be set going. This close association is also seen in the earliest subscription lists. The same people contributed to both, evidently feeling that both missionary society and Bible society were necessary and that the work of the former was impossible or at least seriously handicapped without the latter.

But the association is seen most of all in the day to day activities of both organisations. They have always worked hand in hand. For example, in the sphere of translation, the Bible societies have always been eager to secure the help of missionary linguists, while the missionary societies have always been ready to release their men for this service. It is only necessary to recall such names as Carey and Ziegenbalg in India, Morrison in China, Nommenson in Sumatra, Judson in Burma, Junod in Africa and Bingham in the South Seas to realise how fruitful this co-operation has been. Also in the sphere of distribution the two organisations have worked happily together. The Bible societies have produced the Bible, while the missionary societies have been their best helpers in getting it into the hands of the people. In countless cases, especially in remote areas, mission stations are also Bible depots and centres of Bible distribution. In setting missionaries free for translation work and in encouraging missionaries to take an active part in distributing the Bible, the missionary societies have shown that they regard the Bible as one of the essential tools of their evangelistic and Church-building task.

In all these renewal periods of the Church's life, the Bible played an important part. At the Reformation the Bible stimulated the Reformers by providing them with their message, while the Reformers stimulated the use of the Bible by providing it in a language the people could understand. In the Puritan and Pietist period the Bible came into more general use than ever before, and from that sprang the first evangelistic and missionary ventures of Protestantism. In the period of the Evangelical Revival and the modern missionary movement the Bible and evangelism once again acted and reacted upon one another. The Bible was the agency through which, in the heart of John Wesley, the Evangelical Revival began, while the Evangelical Revival produced the men through whose zeal and devotion the missionary societies were started for sending the gospel to the ends of the earth, and the Bible societies for putting the Bible into the hands of all men everywhere. Each of these renewal periods has gone along with some kind of biblical revival, either a re-discovery of the Bible or a rekindling of interest in its message. Each of the periods has also witnessed the advancement side by side of the Bible cause and evangelistic activity. Finally, each of the periods has provided an illustration of the use of the Bible as a main means of evangelistic growth. Is it too much to say that the enquiry has shown that whenever there has been a rediscovery of the Bible there has also been a revival of evangelistic zeal? It can at least be said that whenever there has been a sustained religious renewal, the Bible has played an important part.

DBWE

III

IN OUR TIME

THE AIM of this chapter is to survey the developments that are taking place in regard to the Bible and evangelism in various parts of the world today. There has been a good deal of study of evangelism in recent years and a number of commissions have been set up both in the Older and in the Younger Churches; there have also been a good many ventures in practical evangelism. Side by side with this there has been a quite remarkable change of attitude in regard to the Bible on the part of practically the whole Christian Church. The question inevitably arises whether there is any connection between the new interest in the Bible and the new concern for evangelism.

A generation ago the Bible suffered general neglect; today there are signs that it is coming into its own again. In the halcyon days of peace and prosperity before the First World War, it was generally thought that the world was getting steadily better; that man was working out his own salvation by education and applied science; that religion was irrelevant or at most a part of the pattern of life that had no particular significance. As for the Bible, it was thought that modern scholarship had undermined its authority and the modern mind dismissed it as out-of-date. The result was that in almost all the older Christian lands it came to be increasingly neglected. Suzanne de Dietrich, summarising a mass of evidence that had been gathered from many countries by the World's Student Christian Federation, said that the Bible had lost its former place in the pulpit, the class-room and the home.[1]

Shortly after the end of the war, however, sensitive minds became aware of a new trend in biblical scholarship. One of the first indications that the tide was beginning to turn was the publication in 1918 of Karl Barth's great commentary on *Romans* with its emphatic assertion that biblical scholarship had got on to the wrong track; that to read the Bible in a merely historical manner, as one would read any other book, was to miss its point altogether. The biblical writers, he affirmed, did not set out to write history in the ordinary sense of the term; they set out to proclaim the good news. Their concern was not so much with what the Jews did, as with what God did through them; and they wrote primarily not to give information but to win man's response. Their aim, as one of their own number said, was that their readers 'might believe that Jesus was the Christ, the Son of God, that believing they might have life through his name.' The Bible should therefore be read as an urgent message to individual men and women, as in fact, 'a message addressed to me with my name on it'.

But in whatever way the biblical renewal may have come about, the important thing is that a new readiness to take the Bible seriously began to show itself. And none too soon!

It came, in fact, just in the nick of time. Who can say what would have happened to the churches of Europe and especially of Germany during the Nazi régime if many of them had not already learnt to listen to God's Word in the pages of the Bible? The Nazi leaders tried to discredit it by stigmatising the Bible as 'a Jewish book', but the Confessing and the Roman Catholic Churches countered by affirming that it was the Church's book and even its sheet-anchor. There

[1] S. de Dietrich, *Le Renouveau Biblique*, 1st edition, p. 14

followed moves and counter-moves. The authorities instructed everyone to read *Mein Kampf*. The churches replied by recommending their people to read the Bible. Bible sales immediately went up and even exceeded those of *Mein Kampf*. The Nazis tightened the screw and carried off church leaders to the concentration camps, but they did not break the power of the Bible. Martin Niemöller continued to read his Bible by such light as his prison window admitted, while Paul Schneider, though brutally beaten, continued to shout verses from the Bible to his fellow-prisoners.[1] It was the Bible that helped them to hold out and that enabled the Church to maintain its resistance in those bitter days.

What was true of Germany was true also of other countries under the Nazi heel. In Norway, during the Quisling régime, the Bible was spoken of as 'the book of the day'. In Holland a resistance paper, printed and circulated clandestinely, said that 'the Bible is the only weapon that can resist the tanks'. In prisoner-of-war camps there was a veritable hunger for the Word of God. In one Oflag there were three Bible study classes going on every week, one on the Old Testament, one on the New Testament and one on the Epistles. In another, a Scottish chaplain, who was himself a prisoner-of-war, said that his 'Bible passed from hand to hand, from morning till evening, and it was booked in advance to be read at this or at that time'.[2] In the little book entitled *Eglises de la Captivité*, issued by the World Committee for Spiritual Aid to Prisoners of War, the part played by the Bible is described with graphic simplicity. In some cases the camp chaplain started a Bible group; in other cases it was one of the prisoners. Many of those who attended the classes were, of course, confessed Christians, but some were complete newcomers and had never

[1] Nathaniel Micklem, *Europe's Book*, p. 17.

[2] S. de Dietrich, *ibid.*, p. 22.

opened a Bible before. In one Stalag a French anarchist from the 'red' area of Paris came across a Bible and was immediately gripped by it. Every evening for three months he sat at the foot of the bed of a fellow-prisoner who had once been a missionary, reading chapter after chapter and asking questions as he went along. At the end of the three months he renounced his atheism and confessed his faith in Christ.[1]

In every country where the Nazis were in control, men turned increasingly to the Bible. They found in it something that strengthened their hearts and stiffened their resistance. It not only helped to keep the Christian faith alive in those dark days, it helped to save Europe.

The ending of the war did not bring the new interest in the Bible to an end. On the contrary, the biblical revival has continued to spread and has made itself felt in various spheres, especially in the theological class-room and the pulpit. All the branches of the Christian Church, Orthodox, Roman and Protestant, both in Europe and overseas, have been affected. In the Protestant world its most marked feature is probably the spread of what has come to be known as Biblical Theology, which is not just a swing of the pendulum back towards the theological orthodoxy and biblical conservatism of an earlier generation. It is a forward rather than a backward move. It does not discard the assured results of biblical research. It accepts them and benefits by them, but it keeps them in their place! The Bible has become again the source-book of theology, and the question now asked about the latest theological publication is not whether 'it meets the demands of the modern mind', but whether 'it does justice to the biblical data'.[2] It is the Bible and the whole Bible that matters. The practice of treating the Old and New Testaments as two

[1] *Eglises de la Captivité*, pp. 75-6.

[2] E. L. Allen, *Religion and Life*, Spring number, 1951, p. 206.

books of different importance and value is now dropped. Instead they are treated as a unity, the one dealing with the preparatory stages of God's redeeming purpose, the other carrying it to its consummation in Christ. The Old Testament by itself is regarded as a sentence left unfinished, while the New Testament by itself as a sentence that has lost its beginning. The whole Bible, from Genesis to Revelation, deals with one theme, namely God's saving purpose in Christ. When this is understood its parts fall into place and its meaning becomes clear.

This biblical renewal has stimulated all kinds of developments, one of the most important being the new activity in the field of translation. In addition to the ceaseless work of the Bible societies in constantly bringing out translations in new languages in the mission field, there has recently been a record output of translations of the Bible in the languages of the older Christian lands. This is true of both the Protestant and the Roman Catholic worlds. Some of them are personal ventures like those of Professor James Moffatt and Monsignor Ronald Knox; others are authorised or approved productions like the Revised Standard Version of America, or the Maredsous Bible of the Belgian Catholics. The appearance of these new translations is a striking proof of the new interest in the Bible in these days, and is at the same time a major contribution towards the task of evangelisation. However much activity there may be in the field of translation, there is even more in that of revision. In every Bible society far more time is being devoted to revising existing versions than to translating the Bible into new languages. Revision is the great task of the moment. There has, in fact, never been a period in the history of Christendom when so many revisions have been in hand. This spate of new revisions is due partly to the fact that scholars now have better texts and fuller linguistic material, partly to growing dissatisfaction with existing versions, partly to the fact that language itself changes in course of time, but mainly to a deep urge to get the gospel across to the common man and with that in view, to put it into a form that everyone can understand. In other words, the motive is primarily evangelistic.

The most phenomenal development in Bible study and Bible circulation is, however, not to be found amongst the well-known branches or denominations of the Christian Church, but amongst the 'sects' on the outer fringe of the Protestant world, especially the Pentecostals, the Seventh Day Adventists, the Jehovah Witnesses and certain other extreme fundamentalist groups. These sects and groups came into being largely as a reaction against the neglect of the Bible and of evangelism, and they are now growing at an astonishing speed and pressing out into every part of the world. They insist that all their members shall take an active part in evangelism and in that propaganda they give a central place to the Bible. An illustration of their activity is seen in a recent evangelistic campaign organised by the Pentecostals in Chile. It not only made a profound impression upon the whole country, but was marked by Bible sales that went far beyond any previous figure. It is this wing of the Church that is buying and circulating the Bible in record numbers, and, significantly enough, it is this wing that is said to be growing more rapidly than any other branch of the Church today. Their method of interpreting the Bible may not commend itself to everyone and they may be more inclined than most to bring their own views to it than to try to discover what the biblical writers intended to say. But putting these objections aside, the fact remains that these extreme sects are probably doing more Bible reading and Bible distribution than any other section of the Christian Church.

So much for developments within the Protestant world. Within the Roman Catholic world the change of attitude in regard to the Bible is even more striking. It is hardly less than a right-about-face. For centuries the official attitude had been to put the main emphasis on the tradition of the Church rather than on the Bible, and to erect the Vulgate or Latin version of the Scriptures above all others. On both these points there has been a dramatic change of front in recent years. In the first place, Papal Encyclicals[1] and other official pronouncements now urge the faithful to make a regular practice of reading the Bible for themselves. It is no longer stigmatised as a 'Protestant book'; it is recommended as something that every good Catholic should read for himself. In the second place the translation of the Scriptures is no longer discouraged. On the contrary, there is now a Pontifical Commission for the encouragement of biblical study set up under the auspices of the Vatican, while leading Roman Catholic authorities in various countries, realising that the Latin Vulgate is necessarily a closed book for the majority of the faithful, are definitely encouraging translations into the everyday speech of the people. The result is a whole crop of new translations, under the official imprimatur, in Belgium, France, Spain, Italy and elsewhere. It must be a long time since there has been so much activity in the Roman Catholic Church connected with the translation, circulation and study of the Bible.

How far this new interest in the Scriptures within the Roman Church is connected with evangelism is difficult to say. The encyclicals themselves seem to urge Bible study as something good in itself and as a valuable means of deepening the spiritual life of the individual believer, rather than as a spur to evangelism. Individual priests, however, especially

[1] E.g. *Divino Afflante Spiritu*, 1943.

those who are engaged in the active propagation of the faith, welcome the new translations as aids in winning converts and instructing catechumens.

In the Orthodox Church, with one important exception, there has been no such dramatic development. For the average Orthodox Christian the Bible is not something that one possesses and studies for oneself so much as something that one hears read in church. This derives, in part, from the fact that the Orthodox Church has its main strength in countries, such as those of Eastern Europe and the Near East, where there has always been a good deal of illiteracy. It derives, in part also, from the fact that the Orthodox Church has rarely encouraged even its literate members to read the Bible for themselves. The Bible is, of course, read regularly in public worship, but in spite of the respect that is paid to it, its reading is secondary to the recital of the liturgy. A number of Patriarchs and Archbishops in the Orthodox Church are beginning to take a new interest in the Bible, but that is not yet true of the Orthodox clergy and people as a whole. The outstanding exception is Greece, where a biblical renewal of a remarkable character has taken place in recent years. This is largely, but not entirely, due to the influence of the Zöe (life) movement which strongly urges the wide use of the Bible by all classes of the Greek people. It prints and distributes its own edition of the New Testament, and it organises Bible study groups in universities, in churches and in prisons. This new interest in the Bible is clearly associated with evangelistic activity. For the Zöe movement, which is almost entirely a lay movement, is largely responsible for the development of evangelism in hospitals and prisons and for the remarkable growth of the Sunday school movement. Thirty years ago there were no Sunday schools in Greece; today there are over three thousand. The basis of the Sunday school teaching courses and of the fruitful evangelistic work in the prisons is entirely biblical.

It may be added, as an additional indication of the new interest in the Bible, that the Study Department of the World Council of Churches has undertaken as one of its main subjects of enquiry 'The Bible and the Church's Message to the World', and has secured the help of a number of leading authorities in various countries on different aspects of this central theme. Groups of scholars are at work on 'The Biblical Doctrine of Work and Vocation' (in Britain), on 'The Biblical Doctrine of Man in Society' (in the U.S.A.) and on 'The Biblical Doctrine of Justice' (in Europe). In addition, associated and sectional studies are going forward on 'The Relation between the Old and New Testament' (in Holland), on 'Scripture and Tradition' (in Switzerland and Germany), and on 'The Bible and Natural Law' (in Heidelberg), while an international group of scholars, brought together by the Study Department, has published a volume on *The Biblical Authority for the Church's Social and Political Message Today*. When, it may be asked, have so many scholars, the world over, concentrated so much attention upon the Bible, especially with a view to finding its message for the contemporary world? Is there anything more revealing of the new turn Christian thought has taken in regard to the Bible during the last generation?

As this brief survey shows, there has been something like a re-birth of interest in the Bible during recent years. One of the most impressive things about it is that it is true of all the great branches of the Christian Church. That has probably not happened before, and it provokes all kinds of stimulating questions. Does it mean, for instance, that some new approach to the problem of unity is being revealed, an approach based on the Bible rather than on the validity of orders and sacraments? Or, alternatively, does it mean that this biblical renaissance is the prelude to some new expansion of the Christian cause? We have already seen that on more than one occasion a rediscovery of the Bible has been the accompaniment, if not the cause, of a new outburst of evangelistic and missionary advance. Is history going to repeat itself? There are plenty of exciting possibilities.

In regard to the first question, the starting-point is that the rediscovery of the Bible is common to all the great branches of the Christian Church. Is this just an interesting coincidence, or has it a bearing on the question of Christian unity? Does it, for example, point to the possibility of a new approach to the ecumenical problem based on biblical rather than ecclesiastical considerations? The mere putting of the question opens up great vistas of opportunity, and points to the possibility, in the not distant future, of new ecumenical ventures more comprehensive than any so far undertaken. If there is a real rediscovery of the Bible, and at the same time a willingness on the part of all the main branches of the Christian Church to listen together to its message, who can say what insights it may yield or to what goal it may lead? There is reason to think that this possibility is worth consideration. At any rate, there is a certain amount of common ground which can provide a starting-point.

All branches of the Church regard the Bible as the source of their faith or, at least, as one of the sources. Separated though they may be by their various traditions and their distinctive *ethos*, they have this in common that they all claim to be 'built on the foundation of the apostles and the prophets, Jesus himself being the chief corner-stone' (Eph. 2.20). However important the traditions are and however different the *ethos* may be, the fact remains that a common foundation exists and is accepted by all.

On the basis of that common foundation, a number of informal meetings and conversations have taken place during recent years, especially between members of the Protestant and Roman Catholic Churches. These exchanges have shown that the Bible offers the possibility of another approach to the problem of unity. The Faith and Order Movement has concentrated upon a study of the varying views held by different Churches in regard to the content of their faith, the status of the ministry, and the ways of worship. That study, which has been going on for some twenty-five years, has yielded important results, but the way is long and the end is not yet in sight. The suggestion is accordingly being made that another avenue should be explored and that consideration should be given to the possibility of a biblical approach to the problem of unity and disunity—unity in Christ and disunity in the Churches. Suzanne de Dietrich argues that 'the experience of ecumenical conferences and of private meetings between Protestants, Catholics and Orthodox always seems to show that a constructive and lasting agreement can be reached only on the foundation of the Word of God'.[1] She adds that although this road will probably be a long one, 'it is the only sure one. It is only as theologians of all denominations humbly and loyally submit their theological systems to the living and efficacious Word of God that it will be possible for them to get beyond their particular points of view and meet one another in the fellowship of the only Lord of the Church.'[2] In regard to the Bible, Protestants and Catholics are probably nearer together than they think, and it is worth remembering that it is not a Protestant but a Roman Catholic writer who says 'Let us give the whole pure Gospel to our pagan masses; it will enter into their soul, and in time it will flower in a culture, different from ours, simpler probably, but

[1] S. de Dietrich, *ibid.*, p. 289.   [2] *Ibid.*, p. 115.

genuinely Christian and marvellously adapted to their mentality. . . . The masses are ready for this preaching of Christ crucified, provided it is given without admixture.'[1] In Protestant, Catholic and Orthodox circles alike there is a real biblical renewal and a genuine discovery of more and more common ground. It is worth considering whether the prosecution of this line of enquiry may not be God's call to His Church today.

It is also worth giving some consideration to the fact that the new interest in the Bible seems to coincide in many places with the new concern for evangelism. This is so in countries as different as Greece, India, Japan, Britain and Brazil. In Greece, as we have seen, the new interest in the Bible marches with a new zeal for evangelism. In India a careful study has recently been undertaken by the National Christian Council of the way in which the gospel can most fruitfully be communicated to the Indian people, having in mind the structure of their society, the traditions of their life and the strength of their Christian church. Experiments are being carried out in adapting Indian methods to Christian purposes, such as that of living together in simplicity and fellowship in an *ashram*, or that of telling the gospel story by song and speech in the manner of the old-time religious minstrels. There are ventures such as Weeks of Witness in which the whole church in an area shares, or Leaflet Evangelism by means of a series of graded leaflets provided for the reader over a number of weeks or months. These ventures have coincided with a deepened interest in the Bible shown particularly in the Church of South India in its new sense of responsibility for the distribution of the Scriptures. In Britain, the new concern for evangelism is seen in such publications as the Church of England's report entitled *Towards the Conversion of England*, or that of the

[1] Abbé Godin, *La France, Pays de Mission*, p. 96.

Church of Scotland called *Into all the World*. In nearly every communion there is deep concern. There have also been large-scale ventures in evangelism such as the Commando Campaigns following the war years, and the Anglican Mission to London in 1949. This new concern for evangelism and these active ventures have coincided in time with the widespread new interest in biblical theology and the new regard in which the Bible is held. In Japan a committee of the National Christian Council, which has been at work for two years hammering out an evangelistic policy for their country, has recently issued its report. Along with the committee's enquiries, practical experiments in evangelism have been carried out, such as an attempt at occupational evangelism, particularly designed to reach industrial workers, and home evangelism aimed at winning the women, or cinema evangelism especially for young people. These enquiries and experiments have taken place during the very time when Japan has been carrying through the greatest campaign of Bible distribution in its history.

A word of warning is probably necessary against exaggerating the magnitude of the biblical renewal and also against jumping too quickly to conclusions.

That there is an important return to the Bible is beyond dispute. What is more, it is one of the most significant religious developments of our time. But it must not be inferred that the return is as yet widespread or general. On the contrary, the Bible is still a largely unknown book to the majority of people, even in countries with a long Christian tradition. What is claimed here is that there is plenty of evidence that in most branches of the Christian Church the Bible is coming back from the periphery of the Church's life into the centre. So far the return-movement has reached only a relatively small company of leaders and scholars. It has not yet reached the man in the pew, much less the man in the street. But the fact that it has reached the man in the theological class-room, the study and the pulpit, is great gain in itself and holds even greater possibilities for the future. It is the importance not the magnitude of the movement that cannot be exaggerated. And its importance lies in the fact that it may well be the prelude to some great new Christian advance. The previous pages have brought evidence to show that the periods of rediscovery of the Bible, or of fairly widespread renewal of interest in it, have either preceded a new Christian forward movement or else gone along with it. It is tempting to argue from this that the present biblical revival is leading on to a new Christian springtime. But that would be going beyond the evidence. All that can be said with confidence is that such a development is not impossible, and that some at least of the necessary conditions are present. It may be that in the providence of God a new springtime is on its way.

A second consideration concerns the fact that biblical renewal and evangelistic advance appear to go together. The previous pages seem to show that a rekindling of interest in the Bible tends to go along with a renewal of active evangelism. Where the Bible is discovered afresh as God's saving word to men, there evangelism seems to develop. It is worth recalling in this connection that many of the greatest evangelists from Chrysostom to Spurgeon and Moody have been keen advocates of Bible study and convinced believers in the place of the Bible in evangelism. It is equally worth recalling that many of the 'sects' on the outer-fringe of Protestantism that take the Bible seriously and base their whole witness upon it, carry on constant and fruitful evangelism. The inference seems to be that successful evangelism needs the accompaniment of an ever-renewed interest in the Bible.

This leads on to a third consideration. Throughout its history the Christian Church has used the Bible as a main instrument of its evangelistic activity. The early Church used it not only to instruct the faithful, but also to evangelise the non-Christians. The Reformers translated it so that all men might read for themselves the message of God's grace. The Puritans and Pietists applied it to daily life and took it with them to the mission field as the means of winning converts to the faith. The Evangelicals founded societies to print it and to distribute it to all men everywhere. This evidence of history is impressive. There were, of course, some periods when the Church used the Bible less than at others, just as there were certain branches of the Church that used other tools besides the Bible. But no other tool has been in use always and in all sections of the Church. It is a fair summary that all through its history, whenever the Church has been engaged in trying to win the outsider and the non-Christian, it has used the Bible as its main instrument. What is more, the times when the Church has gone to its evangelistic task with the Bible open in its hands have been precisely the times when it has won many of its greatest conquests. The Bible has in fact been the cutting-edge of its advance.

IV

ACHIEVEMENTS

ONE OF the best known of the Bible societies often uses as its symbol the emblem of the sower at work in the field. Some of his seed falls by the wayside, some on stony ground, some in a patch of weeds and some on good soil. He can never be sure what will happen to his seed, just as the man who distributes the Bible can never tell what happens to his books. Some books, bought perhaps to get rid of an importunate person at the door, are put away and forgotten. Some, which the purchaser vaguely intended to read some day, are placed on a shelf and left there. Some are given a place of honour on the parlour table and regularly dusted but never read. Some are used as charms or amulets. Some serve as receptacles for paper money. Some are torn up to provide pipe-lighters. Some are just thrown away. But some are read and re-read, and these are like seed in good soil which bring forth thirty, sixty or a hundred fold. It is with this harvest that the present chapter is concerned, the harvest of lives remade and churches planted through the persistent sowing of the Word. The instances that will be given will not deal with the Bible in the redemption of the community, nor with the Bible in the nurture of the individual beyond the point of conversion. To do that would go far beyond the scope of this enquiry and the length of this book.

1. *The Harvest of Lives Remade*

A classic instance in recent years of a man converted through reading the Bible is that of Tokichi Ishii. The story is told with graphic power and simplicity in the little book entitled *A Gentleman in Prison*. Ishii had an almost unmatched record and was as cruel and pitiless as a tiger. In circumstances of fiendish brutality he had murdered men, women and even children, anyone, in fact, who stood in his way. At last he was caught and was in prison awaiting death. While there he was visited by two Canadian women who tried to talk with him through the prison bars. But he merely glowered at them and paid no heed. Eventually they gave him a Bible in the hope that it would succeed where they had failed. Their hopes were more than realised. He began to read, and having started he could not stop. He read on and on, coming eventually to the story of the Crucifixion. It was the words 'Father, forgive them for they know not what they do', that broke him down. 'I stopped', he said, 'I was stabbed to the heart, as if pierced by a five-inch nail. Shall I call it the love of Christ? Shall I call it His compassion? I do not know what to call it. I only know that I believed and my hardness of heart was changed.'[1] Later, when the jailer came to lead the doomed man to the scaffold, he found not the surly, hardened brute he expected, but a smiling, radiant man, for Ishii the murderer had been born again.

This dramatic story does not, of course, stand alone. The archives of Bible societies are full of instances, less striking perhaps, but not less revealing of the part that the Bible often plays in the conversion of individual men and women. Those that follow are but specimens. They are drawn moreover from so many lands and relate to so many types of people that it is clear that the influence of the Scriptures is not confined to one country or one kind of person. There is, for example, the story of Tommer, an educated Mongolian who found himself under the spell of the very words that made a new man of Ishii. Tommer was by nature hard and un-

[1] Caroline Macdonald, *A Gentleman in Prison*, p. 76.

yielding, and when he agreed in 1943 to help two missionaries who were revising the Mongolian New Testament, he did so with a completely closed mind. 'He would elucidate and mark down the words he thought ought to be changed. But if any attempt was made to explain some Bible truth to him a stern look came over his face and he became as hard and cold as steel. In this way the Gospels of Matthew, Mark and Luke were gone through until the thirty-fourth verse of the twenty-third chapter of St. Luke was reached: "Jesus said, 'Father, forgive them for they know not what they do'." Suddenly Tommer seemed to forget all about the two missionaries and, reading the verse over and over again, he burst into tears and going down on his knees said, "O Lord, I see it now; it was all for me". From that day he was a changed man and became a lover of the Bible and one whose witness was moving to hear.'[1] Marshall Broomhall ransacked the correspondence files of the China Inland Mission for information about the part that the Bible played in the evangelisation of China. One of the stories that he rescued from oblivion[2] was of a man who bought a couple of Gospels from a colporteur in the market, and took them home, put them on a bookshelf and forgot about them. Nearly a year later he came across them and began to read. He became so engrossed that he devoted all his spare time to reading and re-reading them, and then announced that he was going to destroy his idols and worship the true God. He had, however, no idea how to do so; but knowing that God was in heaven he went out every morning before breakfast and knelt on the doorstep, where he knocked his forehead three times on the ground before God, and said: 'God, I truly worship Thee. God I truly worship Thee.' This he did for several months until some Christian folk in another town,

[1] W. H. Hudspeth, *The Bible and China*, p. 37.
[2] Marshall Broomhall, *The Bible in China*, p. 161.

hearing about him, came and gave him regular instruction.

A better-known example of conversion following upon the reading of the Bible is that of the proud Confucian scholar of the old school, destined to become one of the evangelists of Central China and known to the world as Pastor Hsi. A man of culture and education, Hsi tended to keep himself aloof. Preaching left him unmoved. Even the personal friendship of the saintly David Hill was not enough to bring him to the point of decision. It was a copy of the Chinese New Testament, left deliberately on his study table, that succeeded where other means failed. He picked it up and with some hesitation opened it and began to read. As he read on and on, and especially as he neared the end of the Gospel narrative, a curtain seemed to be lifted. He seemed to see the Lord and hear His Word. That decided him. He knelt down there and then and acknowledged Christ as his Saviour and Lord. When he stood up again it was to start on a course from which he never turned back.[1]

Books have always been objects of respect and almost of veneration in China. Latin America, on the other hand, has no such tradition, and there the Bible has often been stigmatised as a 'Protestant book' and publicly burnt in the city square; yet it is in Latin America that it has made some of its most remarkable conquests. 'Take it away. I don't want it', said an angry Bolivian business man to the colporteur .who stood at his door. 'It is an evil book.' The colporteur for some reason replied not in Spanish but in Quechua, which happened to be the man's mother tongue. This led to some conversation and eventually to the purchase of a Bible. Knowing that his wife would not approve of what he had done, the business man decided to read the book in secret. So each morning he got up long before anyone else was astir and, going into a

[1] Geraldine Taylor, *Pastor Hsi; one of China's Scholars*, pp. 46-7.

small room at the end of the house, he lit a candle and sat down to read. One morning while he was getting up he heard a rustle, and putting out his hand in the dark he found his wife there already dressed. 'What are you doing up so early?' he asked. 'I'm coming too,' she replied, and together they went to the little room to read and pray. It soon became a regular practice and before long they made the discovery that for both of them all things had become new.

From the neighbouring country of Brazil comes the somewhat similar story of Signor Antonio of Minas. For some time a friend had been urging him to consider the claims of Christ, and eventually had given him a Bible with the request that he would read it. He took it, but no sooner had he done so than some devilish imp within him made him vow to throw it into the fire immediately he reached home. On his arrival there he found that the fire was out! He relit it and opened the book so that it might the more easily catch alight. It happened to open at the Sermon on the Mount. He paused for a moment to glance at it. The words had in them something that held him. He read on, forgetful of time, through the hours of the night, and just as the dawn was breaking he stood up and declared, 'I believe'.[1]

Vincente Quiroga of Chile had an equally transforming experience. In his case it followed upon the seemingly chance discovery of a few pages of a book amongst the debris that had been washed up on the beach after an earthquake. He picked up the pages, spread them out and dried them in the sun. Then he sat down and tried to read them. He found that they contained the strangest message he had ever come across. He read them again and again, becoming more and more fascinated and at the same time more and more bewildered. He took the pages home and showed them to a friend, who

[1] *American Bible Society Report*, 1951, p. 228.

suggested that they might perhaps have come from a book called 'the Bible' which he had heard a missionary speaking about in Santiago not long before. Quiroga tracked the missionary down, showed him his precious pages, and came away with a complete Bible under his arm. The book soon did its work and Quiroga not only became a Christian, but dedicated himself for the rest of his life to distributing Scriptures in the neglected villages of northern Chile.[1]

From Chile to Cambodia is a far cry, but in both countries the Bible has the same evangelising power. In the case of Chile the man concerned was a young business man, in that of Cambodia it was an ex-Buddhist priest who had been employed to teach the language to some newly-arrived missionaries. The prescribed course included learning to read the Gospels in the phonetic script, which the missionaries did not understand but which the ex-priest did. He disliked the task intensely, for he despised all forms of religion and regarded the missionaries as engaged on a foolish and futile enterprise; but he kept at it. Before long the story began to cast its spell over him. He started asking questions; he took to reading the book not for the missionaries' sake but for his own. He just could not let the book alone. For five months he read it and for five months he withstood its claims. Then he gave in. He asked for instruction, accepted baptism and was duly enrolled as a Christian believer.[2]

The case of John Subhan, now a Bishop of the Methodist Church in North India, is even more remarkable, not only because he was a loyal Moslem, but also because he was a strict member of the Sufi sect. As a boy he attended a Moslem school, studied the Koran under the direction of the mullah, and lived

[1] Eugene Nida, *God's Word in Man's Language*, p. 166.

[2] Eric Fenn, *Not by Bread Alone*, p. 12 (Report of British and Foreign Bible Society 1952).

in an entirely Moslem setting. He had no associations of any
kind with Christian people or Christian institutions. To the best
of his knowledge he had never met either a missionary or an
Indian pastor. He had never heard a Christian address and had
certainly never listened to a Christian sermon. But he had read a
Gospel! Just one! 'It was sufficient', he said. 'It convinced me
and I decided to become a Christian.' There was apparently no
other agency at work except the single Gospel. It is that simple
fact, or something like it, that stands out in all these cases.

Put beside the gentle-mannered John Subhan, brought up
with such cloistered care, the New York gangster and ex-
convict recently in prison for burglary with violence. It
would be difficult to find two men more different. One a
quiet but determined man with a religious turn of mind, the
other a violent rebel against society. Yet different as they were,
the Bible had its way with both of them. Moreover, in both
cases it was apparently the only agent at work. The ex-
convict was in fact on his way to join his old gang with a
view to another burglary when he picked a man's pocket in
Fifth Avenue, New York, and slipping into Central Park
to see what he had acquired, found himself in possession of a
New Testament. Having time to spare before joining his
comrades, he sat down and began to read. Soon he was deep
in the book, and he read to such effect that a few hours later
he went to his comrades and told them bluntly what he had
been doing, and broke with them for good. Once again the
Bible was the instrument, and to all appearances, the only
instrument of the man's remarkable and right-about change.

Almost as dramatic is the story of a violent young Arab in
Aleppo, who had had a bitter quarrel with a former associate.
'I had made up my mind to kill him', he confessed recently
to a Bible society colporteur. 'I hated him so much that I
plotted revenge, even to the point of murder. Then one day

I ran into you and you induced me to buy a copy of St. Matthew. I only bought it to please you. I never intended to read it. But as I was going to bed that night the book fell out of my pocket and I picked it up and started to read. When I reached the place where it says, "Ye have heard that it was said by them of old time, Thou shalt not kill. . . . But I say unto you that whosoever is angry with his brother without a cause shall be in danger of the judgment", I remembered the hatred I was nourishing against my enemy. As I read on my uneasiness grew until I reached the words, "Come unto me all ye who labour and are heavy laden, and I will give you rest. Take my yoke upon you, and learn of me; for I am meek and lowly in heart; and ye shall find rest unto your souls." Then I was compelled to cry: "God be merciful to me a sinner." Joy and peace filled my heart and my hatred disappeared. Since then I have been a new man and my chief delight is to read God's Word.'[1] With this would-be murderer in Aleppo as with the gangster in New York, it was the reading of the Scriptures, and as far as one can tell it was that alone, that suddenly diverted him from his course of violence and hatred and set his feet in a new path.

'Take this and read it', said a Japanese schoolgirl as she handed a dirty, little booklet to a woman standing at her door. 'I found it in the street. Somebody must have dropped it.' The girl knew that the woman had been left a widow with three small children, that she had sought comfort at the Shinto shrine, that she had been to the Buddhist priest, that she had made a long pilgrimage, but all in vain; her grief had not been assuaged. 'I read it', continued the girl. 'There is a wonderful story in it of a man who helps those who are helpless. I thought of you; it might do you good.' The woman took the booklet. It was a copy of St. Luke's Gospel in

[1] Eric Fenn, *Not by Bread Alone*, p. 25.

Japanese. She read it from beginning to end without stopping and she knew that for the rest of her life she could go only in the direction which the booklet had shown her. Her first action was to try and find if there were any other Christians in the neighbourhood, but though she made enquiries far and wide she found none. One day, however, in the near-by market town, she heard a missionary speaking about *Iesa Kirisuto*. She went up and asked him to come to her mountain village and visit her home. A few weeks later she was baptised, and in the course of a few months her village had a small congregation of those who had found faith in Christ through 'the Book'.[1] Here again it was the book and the book only that was the means of the woman's conversion. Her meeting with the missionary, her instruction in the faith and her baptism came later. It was the book that was the instrument of the deep change in her life.

A final illustration of a more humdrum character must suffice to complete this group of witnesses to the evangelistic power of the Bible. It comes from a Ward Sister in a children's hospital in England. She had been finding life, as she herself said, futile and meaningless. 'I sought desperately for an answer to the riddle of it all. For almost a year my search continued. I waded despairingly through philosophy after philosophy. I was hindered from reading the Scriptures by the arguments of a friend, who convinced me that the Bible could not possibly be true. But one day some good soul brought to the hospital a supply of Gospels for the use of the patients. I was constrained to take a copy of St. John's Gospel and read it through for myself. I read it avidly, and as I read all arguments fell away. It shone and glowed with truth, and my whole being responded to it. The words that finally decided me were those in John 18.37, "To this end was I born and for this cause came I into the world, that I should bear witness unto the

[1] Eric Fenn, *Not by Bread Alone*, p. 17.

truth. Everyone that is of the truth heareth my voice." So I listened to that voice and heard the truth and found my Saviour.'[1]

These twelve examples have been chosen out of the multitude available, and not from a limited field but from a dozen different countries and as many different walks of life. They range from a Japanese murderer to an English nurse, from a Confucian scholar to a New York gangster, from a Buddhist priest to a Bolivian business man, from a tragic Japanese widow to a sheltered Moslem youth, from a Mongolian linguist to a Chilean townsman, from a fiery Arab to a quiet Chinese peasant. These examples cover such a wide variety that it is impossible to brush them aside as exceptional or as having no significance. The fact is that in this wide variety there are two features that are constant, namely the influence of the Scriptures and the change in human lives. These features occur so regularly that the examples cited cannot be dismissed as freaks or rarities. Ever since there has been a Bible, men have been converted by reading it; from Tatian and Justin Martyr to the present day. And they have been converted in almost every country where the Bible has been translated into the vernacular. This has not, of course, been the only way in which converts have been won; but it has always been one of the ways, and one of the most fruitful ways, that God has used.

At times, the actual words of the Bible read aloud have been the means, under God, of moving men's hearts and making a revolution in their lives. One of the notable instances of this is the story of a colporteur[2] who was held up at the point of a revolver in a Sicilian forest at dead of night and ordered to light a bonfire and burn his books. Having lit the fire he asked if he might read a brief extract from each book before consigning it to the flames. From one he read the 23rd Psalm; from

---

[1] *Scripture Gift Mission Report*, 1952, pp. 20-1.

[2] Edwin W. Smith, *God's Packmen*, pp. 29 *seq.*

another the Parable of the Good Samaritan; from another the Sermon on the Mount; from another Paul's hymn to love, and so on. After the reading of each extract the brigand exclaimed: 'That's a good book; we won't burn that one; give it to me.' In the end not a book was burned. They passed one by one into the brigand's hands, who went off, books and all, into the darkness. Years later he turned up again, but this time as an ordained Christian minister, and telling his story to the colporteur he said: 'It was the reading of your books that did it.'

In countless cases the mere reading of the Bible has cast a spell over people, even over the most unlikely ones. John Wesley tells in his *Journal* how the rough, untamed miners of Kingswood stopped their raucous shouting as he read the words of Scripture to them. Dr. Turner of Buenos Aires describes in his book *La Biblia en America Latina*, how on more than one occasion a torrent of invective has been checked and turned to words of goodwill by the mere reading of some Bible passage. This sometimes happens even in the hostile atmosphere of a Moslem land. A Bible Society agent says that he has often gained a hearing for the gospel by going boldly into a café and reading aloud a Bible story in colloquial Arabic. He has found that the story of the Prodigal Son is sure to be listened to. Other favourites are the Parables of the Sower and the Lost Sheep. 'Again and again', he says, 'hands have been thrust out and a coin exchanged for a Gospel.'[1]

It is almost impossible, as it has already been said, for those who distribute the Bible to know what happens to the books they sell. And this, of course, makes it difficult to get reliable data about the Bible and conversion. Colporteurs, for example, by the very nature of their calling, have to cast their bread upon the waters and hope that it will return, perhaps after many days. How is it possible for them to keep track of a

[1] *National Bible Society of Scotland Report*, 1951, p. 23.

contact made in an Eastern bazaar, or of a New Testament sold to a pilgrim at a festival, or of a Gospel that changes hands following a conversation in a train? However careful colporteurs are to hand on information about their contacts to the nearest church folk, there are bound to be multitudes of contacts that are never heard of again. Even a man who travels about less than a colporteur does, finds it hard to keep track of those to whom he hands on the Scriptures. The buyer is often just one in a crowd; he may even be a stranger from another town. He buys his book and goes his way. It is almost impossible to know what he does with his book or into whose hands it eventually gets. No one knows, to take an example, how the Bible came into the hands of Wadé Harris of the Ivory Coast in West Africa. But however it happened and whoever was the agent, this one Bible in the hands of an African layman led to one of the most remarkable evangelistic movements of the century.

Carrying a cross in one hand and a Bible in the other, the Prophet Harris, as he was called, travelled about the countryside, declaring his simple message. He would enter a village, hold up his Bible and declare, 'I proclaim the Word of the Lord'. When questioned about his authority, he would point to the book and say: 'The Word of the Lord says, "Go and teach all nations". I am the Watchman in his book. I cry, "Prepare ye, prepare ye".' He never referred to any connection with a mission or a missionary; he merely referred to the book. It was that that set him going, that gave him his message and that enabled him to lead tens of thousands of his fellow-countrymen to Christ.[1]

If those who distribute the Bible always knew what happened to their books and what results followed, what a story it would be! It would certainly show that the Bible has had

[1] W. J. Platt, *An African Prophet*, p. 52.

a greater share in winning converts and planting churches than most people realise. As it is, with the very partial knowledge that is available, the story is one of the most impressive in the growth of the Christian Church. Dr. Christy Wilson, speaking out of wide experience of Moslem countries, says that he was surprised to find how many Moslems had become Christians through reading the Bible as compared with the number converted through preaching, educational or even medical work. 'In asking Christians, who had formerly been Moslems, what first attracted their attention to Christ and what finally brought about their conversion, I observed that in a large majority of cases the Bible had much to do with the process.'[1] Even when the Bible is denounced and when people are warned against it, it still seems to have a strange, converting power. 'If you read that book', said a young Brazilian to his friend who had bought a Bible, 'you will change your religion and desert your father's faith.' When they met again a few months later, the young man said: 'Well, I read the book and gave it to my father who also read it. We have both accepted its teaching. We are believers in Jesus and do not have to change anything except our lives.'[2]

One of the impressive facts about the Bible in relation to evangelism is that its influence rarely stops with the individual. When a man finds new life through the Bible he almost invariably shares his discovery with someone else, perhaps with several others. Signor Miegge recently found this happening, of all unlikely places, within the confines of a Roman prison. A man who was serving a thirty years' sentence and was known to be a hard case, was given a Bible by a fellow-prisoner who was leaving the jail. He read it

[1] Christy Wilson, 'The Bible and Moslems' in *The Moslem World*, July 1937, p. 237.

[2] *British and Foreign Bible Society Report*, 1951, p. 59.

and, as he himself said, the reading changed his life. 'I was loud in my curses', he wrote, 'I was a hard materialist and a corrupt man. Now all that is changed. In the eyes of the world I am still a bad man, but in the eyes of God I am a new-born creature.' Unable to keep his new-found joy to himself, he devised ways of sharing his experience with his fellow-prisoners. He managed to get Bibles for them, and he did his best to guide their reading and to tell them what it meant. He became a kind of apostle in prison, and today there is a little group of Christian believers behind those prison doors.[1]

Not less striking in its way is the story that Johnson Roe of the British and Foreign Bible Society delights to tell. Travelling in Spain just before the Civil War he met a woman who told him that one day when she was a young girl working in the fields, a colporteur passed by. He offered a Gospel to one of the men, whose only response was to abuse him and throw the Gospel into the ditch. The colporteur moved on, but the Gospel floated down to a point near where the girl was working. Out of curiosity she rescued it, took it home, dried it and later on read it. It was a copy of St. John's Gospel. She read it a second time; then she read it to her family; and after that she read it to her neighbours. Gradually a little group formed a habit of coming on Sundays to hear it read. In due time they built a place for their meetings and formed themselves into an evangelical church.

The impulse to tell others is also illustrated in a recent story from the Yucatan peninsula in Mexico. A few years ago a man, Don Gerardo by name, while wandering along the streets of Merida, noticed a battered book lying on the top of a heap of rubbish. It had no covers and had lost a good many pages, but he picked it up and out of curiosity began to read. He soon found that it was a different kind of book from

[1] Eric Fenn, *Not by Bread Alone*, p. 69.

any that he had come across before. The more he read the more interested he became, and when the message began to lay hold of his heart he decided to take it back to his home fifty miles away. On arriving there he began to talk about the book and the information it contained. By great good fortune a colporteur came to the village a few days later and told Don Gerardo that the book he had found was the Bible, the book in which God speaks to men. Don Gerardo eagerly drank in all that the colporteur could tell him, and later he shared it with his friends. When the colporteur had gone a few of them began to meet from time to time to read the book together, and to discuss its meaning. That went on until towards the end of 1952 when two missionaries came that way and held a service, at the close of which some sixty men and women, including the village mayor, came forward and declared their desire to follow Christ.[1]

These stories can be paralleled a hundred times by authentic accounts drawn from almost every part of the world. What happened in these instances was remarkable, but it was not unique; it was not even so very unusual. Something like it has happened so often and under such varying conditions that a saying has become current amongst those concerned with Christian growth; it is that there is first a Bible, then a convert, then a church. The section that follows will serve to illustrate how frequently this sequence has come true.

2. The Harvest of Churches Planted

However impressive it may be that the Bible has often been the instrument of the conversion of individuals, it is even more impressive that it has been used to bring whole churches and communities into being. It may be possible to find a way of explaining individual conversions as being due

[1] *The Presbyterian World*, June 1953, pp. 78-9.

not merely to the influence of the Bible, but to such factors as the continuing impressions of childhood days, the unremembered words of friends long ago, and the unquestioned power of intercessory prayer. But it is not so easy to explain the existence of a worshipping group or an organised congregation. There is something too objective, too solid, even too stolid, about groups, to dismiss them as the fruit of subconscious functionings. What is more, groups that claim a Bible origin are to be found in almost every part of the world. They are not a local phenomenon, due to influences at work in one particular area or kind of society; they are to be found amongst people everywhere.

Evidence of the part that the Bible has played in church planting is so abundant that a selection will have to be made. It will perhaps be best to look first of all at a number of instances of church planting on a large scale, and then to turn to a few cases of a more modest character. Good examples of large-scale expansion in which the Bible has played a leading part are found in Latin America, Madagascar, Korea and Formosa. These areas are so markedly different from one another that it is difficult to find any common factor. The peoples concerned have different racial origins, possess different types of social organisation, and have followed different paths of historical development. Yet for all their differences they are alike in one respect. They all have large and vigorous Christian communities whose emergence and growth have been closely linked with the Scriptures. This will be borne out in the following paragraphs.

In Latin America the Bible societies were early in the field, and in hundreds of places people met for Bible reading long before they even thought of becoming a regular congregation or seeking a pastor. It is, in fact, difficult to exaggerate the part that the Bible has played in planting and nurturing churches in that continent. 'It is no legend', writes Dr.

Turner of Buenos Aires, 'that literally scores and scores of present-day strong evangelical churches in Latin America sprang up and came into existence around a copy of the Word of God. . . . The villager or townsman who secured a copy, read it and later called in a friend to read it with him. Then other neighbours were interested until a large group would come together regularly as a kind of fellowship to read the Word, and a Christian nucleus would be formed without contact with any outside religious movement.'[1]

No one can travel much in Latin America without coming upon church after church that had its origin in some group that first met for Bible reading. The Brazilian town of Manaos offers a good illustration. Fifty years ago a business man in the town bought a wheelbarrow full of Bibles from a man who stopped at his shop door. He did not sell them; that would have roused opposition; he loaned them to anyone who asked to borrow. For years there was no Christian witness in the town, apart from those books, and no missionary ever came. Then the Bible-readers began to meet together and today there are five churches in Manaos, each fully self-supporting and each with its own Brazilian pastor.

Few people can speak with greater authority on this subject than F. C. Glass, the veteran colporteur in Brazil. He writes: 'In dozens of places where I sold the first copies of the Scriptures the people ever saw, there are strong evangelical churches today.'[2] In a recent personal interview he added: 'It was almost invariably the case that the Bible was first on the scene, then later came the preacher, except in those cases where the colporteur being also an evangelist, the Bible and the preacher came together. I cannot recall a single case when the Bible came second. Speaking from personal experience

[1] C. W. Turner, *La Biblia en America Latina*, p. 105.
[2] F. C. Glass, *Through the Heart of Brazil*, p. 145.

I should therefore say that if you want to open up a new area the first thing to do is to send in someone with a Bible.'

In what is called the Coffee Mountain area of Brazil there is today a well-organised and active church. It traces its origin to a few Bibles sold by an illiterate negro who passed that way some thirty years ago. He could not read, but his heart had been set on fire by the message of the Bible and he devoted himself to bearing his witness and selling the book to any who would buy. His testimony was so moving that several of the farmers bought copies, and as time went by they began to talk to one another about what they read. This led to their meeting occasionally to read the Bible together and to discuss it, which in turn led to the holding of Sunday services. All this took place without any contact with any outside person or group. Years later this little community, of about 150 people all told, linked themselves to the Independent Presbyterian Church of Brazil.[1]

An equally remarkable story comes from Peru. Towards the end of 1936 a rumour went round amongst the Protestants in Lima that in an up-country area four groups of people were meeting regularly for Bible study, but had only one Bible between them! A visit was arranged, and it was discovered that these four groups had come into being through reading a copy of a Bible which had been found in an old trunk. How it got there no one knew. All that was known was that when it was found it was handed round and read by one person after another, and in time four groups began to meet to study it in turn. These four groups were afterwards formed into four evangelical congregations, and still later they became the nucleus of a properly constituted Presbytery.[2] Many of the churches of Peru were, like this one, little more

[1] J. A. Mackay, *That Other America*, p. 151.
[2] J. Ritchie, in a letter dated 1st July, 1947.

than Bible-reading groups in the first instance. Having been formed through the ministry of the printed page, and there being no Christian worker available to minister to them, except on rare visits, they have learned to depend upon the reading of the Bible as a means of grace. 'In one extreme case, a small group of Christians came into being through one man learning to read by means of the Bible, and then reading it to others. The Bible was literally the leader's reading primer, and was spiritually the A.B.C. of salvation to the rest of them. It was through the book that the leader had learned to read and it was through that same book that they had come to experience salvation through faith in Jesus Christ. The book brought them together and held them together.'[1] Instances of this kind could easily be multiplied, but they would only say at length what Dr. John Mackay has said briefly in his book *The Other Spanish Christ*, that 'the Bible was the pioneer of the evangelical movement in Latin America.'

Madagascar has always been regarded as providing one of the clearest demonstrations of the place of the Bible in the growth and extension of the Christian Church. After an inauspicious start, the Christian enterprise struck its roots in Malagasy soil and began to grow. It grew so rapidly that it roused opposition, and the reigning Queen put herself at the head of a movement which had the deliberate intention of wiping it out. First of all the missionaries were banished and when they were out of the way, the persecution of the Malagasy Christians began. But though the missionaries were driven out, the Bible was left behind and as the persecution became more bitter the Bible became more and more precious. Christians refused to give it up, though its possession meant death. They hid their copies in rice pits, hollow trees and mountain caves. They even took them to pieces and sewed

[1] J. H. Twentyman, in a letter dated 3rd January, 1947.

the separate pages into the linings of their garments. Sometimes on dark nights a few of them would make their way into the wilds and there, deep in the recesses of a cave, they would light a torch and read their precious books. If they were caught the penalty was death, but that did not deter them. For twenty-five years they faced the persecution with the Bible as their only visible aid. They were burnt at the stake; they were thrown from the hurling rocks; they were speared to death; but the church not only survived, it grew, and when the persecution ended there were some thousands more Christians in the land than when it began. This is perhaps the classic case of a church that owes its life to the Bible.[1]

Another outstanding example is that of Korea which, as the Tambaram Report says, 'is a modern miracle; in 1885 not one believer; in 1938, 380,000'. At the heart of this remarkable growth is the regular study of the Bible. 'Every one of the 3,000 churches', to quote the Tambaram Report again, 'has a Bible class at least once and sometimes twice every year.'[2] These classes usually last a week. Three or four hours each morning are given to Bible study in groups; the same hours each afternoon are devoted to personal evangelism and visitation, while the evenings are kept for evangelistic meetings. Something like half the members of the church join these classes every year. In addition there are Bible Institutes that run for six or eight consecutive weeks, and Bible correspondence courses for those who prefer to study at home. No wonder that the Tambaram Report says that 'the Bible is the centre of everything in the Korean Church'.[3] In few parts of the world has there been a church more alive to its evangelistic task. Since the beginning of the century there have been four great evangelistic movements, and in

[1] J. A. Patten and Edward Shillito, *The Martyr Church.*
[2] *Tambaram Report Vol. IV*, p. 155.   [3] *Ibid.,* p. 161.

each case those movements had their origin in meetings for Bible study and intercession. One of them began when 'a group of missionaries met in Wonsan for Bible study and prayer'.[1] Another followed upon 'the annual 10-day Bible class in Pyengyang'.[2] In the first, which went on for three years, the number of Christians was doubled. In the second, it was nearly trebled. Speaking about these evangelistic or revival movements at the Edinburgh Conference in 1910, Dr. Moffett, a Korea missionary, said: 'It is my profound conviction that what has contributed most to the spiritual transformation of the Koreans and what has made the Korean Church a missionary Church, is the vast organisation of Bible study groups. . . . These groups are true generators of spiritual power that spreads itself through the whole Church.'[3] Dr. Wasson adds the comment that these revivals were not only born in Bible study and prayer, but that their continued fruitfulness seemed to depend upon the continuance of that study and prayer. One of the four revival movements, he says, had disappointing results, and he adds that that was probably due to the fact that the Bible classes and prayer meetings were allowed to lapse. In his stimulating study called *The Growing Edge of the Church*, Dr. Raymond Dudley is led to a similar conclusion in regard to the mission field as a whole. He says, as a result of his enquiries, that 'the enduring value of striking revivals will depend in a large measure upon establishing and maintaining real Bible study.'[4]

Turning to Formosa, recent happenings there have been described as constituting 'one of the most remarkable movements in modern missions'.[5] The writer, who tells the story

[1] A. W. Wasson, *Church Growth in Korea*, p. 30.   [2] *Ibid.*, p. 52.
[3] *Edinburgh Missionary Conference Report*, 1910.
[4] R. Dudley, *The Growing Edge of the Church*, p. 7.
[5] Edward Band, *He Brought Them Out*, p. 3.

of those movements, says: 'During the recent world war an underground Christian movement broke out amongst the mountain tribes of Formosa in spite of all efforts by the Japanese police to suppress it. When the missionaries returned to the island after the war they found to their amazement that some 7,000 of these aborigines, whose forefathers had been head-hunters, had become Christians.'

The first indication that anything was afoot was when the Japanese authorities found large numbers of Bibles being sent up-country. Orders were issued to intercept them and to confiscate any that were found. The result of this order was the organisation of a system of smuggling Bibles into the mountains through the Japanese lines. Sometimes the smugglers were caught and severely punished, but they were not deterred. 'You can cut off our limbs if you like', said one of them, 'but our hearts will be Christian still'.

There were two leaders of the movement, an elderly woman and a young man, both of whom had had a course of training in a Bible school and had become evangelists to their own people. The method they adopted in their evangelistic work was to get small groups of people together and give them Bible instruction. The method caught on and began to spread until there was a real Bible movement. The Japanese, fearing that it might have some political significance, tried to stamp it out, but they only succeeded in driving it underground. As their grip tightened, the Bible meetings had to be more and more secret, the leaders of the little groups having to devise ways of keeping the movement going and at the same time keeping out of the clutches of the Japanese. From time to time little groups of mountain people would creep down the valleys under cover of night, slip past the police cordons, and make their way to a house where a Christian teacher lived. They would rouse him from his sleep with the request: 'Teacher, please give us a Bible lesson. We have only half an hour to spare, for we must be back home by day-break.' For half an hour they had their Bible class, then their lesson over, they would slip back to the mountains, carrying with them a few more crumbs of the gospel to share with their folk at home. Missionary help was out of the question, for during the Japanese occupation missionaries had had to withdraw. From the first it was an indigenous movement carried on by the people themselves. The two leaders had many narrow escapes, and the young man was eventually caught, but the woman continued her work until the Japanese collapse. The result of the movement was not fully seen until the end of the war, for when the missionaries returned they found that thousands had become Christians and were waiting to be received into the Church: the fruit of the work of two humble, ill-trained workers with only the Bible in their hands.

Latin America, Madagascar, Korea and Formosa are outstanding illustrations of the place of the Bible in church-planting and development. They are large-scale examples and concern large numbers of people. Over and above these are plenty of other examples in which only small groups of people are involved, as the next few paragraphs will show.

In a remote village in North-West China, Miss Cable and her colleagues the Misses French, sold a Gospel to a man named Yang. He could not read but he took the book home and put it aside. Later his brother, paying a visit to the house, found the Gospel and read it. It interested him so deeply that he determined to learn more about the Christian faith. Finally he was converted and became the means of the con-version of his brother and his household. Bitter opposition followed for them all, but they stood their ground and won over their neighbours one by one. Though they were des-perately poor and never far from the starvation line, they managed between them to put up a little building to serve as a place of worship for the forty or fifty people who regularly gathered from the scattered homesteads around. It was the printed Gospel that gave them their start.[1]

It was something even more primitive than Yang's mud-walled chapel that a traveller in East Africa came upon in 1951. In a clump of trees near the road he found a few trunks of trees propped up to serve as benches ranged in front of a rude lectern or reading-desk. In a few minutes a handful of villagers arrived, took their places at the benches and under the leadership of one of their number, who stood at the lectern, a service began. The leader was not an evangelist; he wasn't a teacher; he wasn't appointed or paid by anyone; he was just a village Christian. His brother had given him a Zande New Testament and he began to read this not only to himself but also to his neighbours. Before long they formed a habit of meeting together to read the Bible, or hear it read. Their next step was to have a place of meeting, and between them they put up some benches and made a lectern, and there from Sunday to Sunday they met to hear the Word of God as their leader read to them from the New Testament and explained it as best he could.

In this case God used a young man who had a New Testament in his hand. In the next case, He used a little slave girl with equally remarkable results.

Rather more than fifty years ago a young Malagasy woman of a slave-owning family was doing business in the slave-market at Mandritsara in northern Madagascar. As she was looking somewhat critically at a group of slaves that were for sale, her attention was caught by one amongst them, a little southern girl who for some reason said to her, 'Buy me! Please buy me!' The purchase was completed and the mistress returned to her home with the little slave-girl following

[1] *National Bible Society of Scotland Report*, 1947, p. 59.

quietly behind. In the days that followed, this stranger in a strange land relieved her loneliness by reading the one book she had—a Malagasy New Testament. Her mistress, surprised to find her with a book, asked: 'Can you read?' 'Yes,' replied the girl, 'can't you?' 'No', was the reply, 'can you teach me?' There and then the mistress sat down and had her first lesson in reading. She learnt quickly and soon the book began to make its impression. The mistress invited others to join in the reading, and before long a little company of seekers gathered round the slave-girl and a church was ready to be born. In time it was born, and a vigorous and growing church exists in Mandritsara today, with daughter churches in the surrounding countryside.

This miracle, or something like it, is being repeated in many places and it can be seen even where churches are not yet in being, but are only at the pre-natal stage. In Turkey, religious work is carried on under a completely secularised régime. For thirty years open evangelism has been impossible, and in many places what religious life there was had slowly petered out, and a generation has grown up that knows little or nothing of religion of any kind.

A few years ago a keen young colporteur decided to visit a village in the far south-west of Turkey, not far from the Syrian border, where no evangelist or colporteur had been for many years. 'Come by all means', the people wrote in response to his enquiry about the advisability of a visit, 'but don't expect to sell any books, for none of us can read.' On his arrival he found a handful of people who still called themselves Christians, retained some memories of their early Christian instruction, but had long ceased to meet for worship or prayer. He went into their homes and wherever he could do so, he read the Bible to them and prayed. He even sold some books and taught them a few hymns. 'And now', as the colporteur wrote, 'there is a movement amongst these villagers to establish some sort of regular Christian worship.'[1] In this case the Bible was the instrument used to reopen a door that had become closed; and in a country like Turkey, with its secular régime, it is almost the only instrument that can be used. Open-air preaching or indeed any kind of public advocacy of Christianity is out of the question. The only religious activity that is permissible has to be private and within doors. In a situation of this kind the Bible is far and away the best ally the evangelist can have.

The final illustration comes from Kenya, in East Africa, where Christians have been subjected to heavy pressure from the Mau Mau organisation. A good many Christians have left the Church, but of those who have stood firm, even to the point of martyrdom, most have been 'revival Christians', as they are called. They are the fruit of 'a movement that started twenty years ago when a few Africans decided to read their Bibles with expectancy and with complete willingness to obey the Word which might come to them. It has spread to a good many parts of Central and East Africa, setting men and women singing with joy and a sense of new power. In recent months, in Kikuyuland, the test has come. To refuse the Mau Mau oath is practically to sign your own death warrant; to remain loyal to the Church is to invite persecution; to be a Christian has become, of a sudden, to stand in mortal peril. For these "revival Christians" it is not a matter merely of loyalty to government; it is a matter of obedience to the living God.'[2]

These instances, drawn from a wide field, will suffice to show that in the planting and nurturing of churches, as well as in the conversion of individuals, the Bible has played a large and indispensable part. It is doubtful whether any other single factor has had so large a share in the growth of the Church since the Bible societies came into existence.

[1] *American Bible Society Report*, 1950, p. 222.
[2] Eric Fenn, *Not by Bread Alone*, p. 33.

Part Two

USING THE BIBLE
IN EVANGELISM
TODAY

IN THIS PART of the book an attempt will be made to show the way in which the Bible is used in present-day evangelistic activity. Examples, drawn from various parts of the world, will be given showing the precise manner in which the Bible is used, how it helps in various types of work and how the very process of distribution has evangelistic results. An attempt will also be made to consider the different methods adopted with a view to discovering which ones, in actual experience, prove to be most fruitful. The next two chapters will be devoted to this. The first will be concerned with the way in which individual workers, such as colporteurs or those engaged in personal evangelism, use the Scriptures; the second will deal with the use of the Bible in concerted efforts such as campaigns, Bible weeks, exhibitions and home mission drives.

V

USING THE BIBLE IN INDIVIDUAL WORK

'HERE is the very thing you need.' The words spoken in a clear, strong voice, made everyone in the railway coach turn towards the speaker and listen. Some of the passengers recognised him at once, for he often travelled on that train. He was a colporteur, John of the Cross by name, who made a practice of selling Scriptures on the suburban trains of Rio de Janeiro. He had worked out a technique of Bible selling so planned that in the course of a suburban journey he would spend a few minutes in each coach. If the train was made up of eight coaches and the journey took forty minutes, he knew that he would be able to give about five minutes to each coach.

On this particular day he waited till the train pulled up at the first station, and there was a brief respite from the noisy rattle of the wheels on the rails. Then taking his stand at the end of the coach he began to speak loudly enough for all to hear. 'Here is the very thing you need', he began, holding up what looked like an illustrated magazine. 'Carnival is over now and Easter is approaching. This is the period in which to prepare your hearts and minds, and this book will help you to prepare better than anything else in the world. For this book tells what God has done for us all. It tells the story of the angel's announcement to the Blessed Virgin Mary; it tells of the birth of Jesus, of His infancy, of His home in Nazareth. It tells of His life and teaching, of His death and resurrection. It is all here in this book and there are pictures too. Pictures of the places where Jesus was born and brought up, where He was crucified for our sake, and where He rose again.

This is the book you need. Buy it and you buy a blessing. And here on the back my name and address are stamped, so that if you care to write to me you can do so, or if you would like to come and talk to me I am always at home on Saturdays.'

Then he began selling, walking down the length of the coach as he did so. The price per copy was the same as the cost of two newspapers, so that it was cheap enough. Men and women alike bought and in all about eight or nine copies were sold. In a few cases people put questions to him, and he stopped for a moment or two to answer them and to explain more fully what the Gospel was about.

Just as the train was slowing down for the next station he stepped across the connecting way to the next coach. As soon as the train stopped he began his talk once more. It took about two minutes, not more, and was in very similar terms to his brief message in the first coach. Here again he sold a number of copies and had a brief chat with one or two individuals before the train began to slow down once more, and he passed on to the third coach. And so it went on until he had gone the whole length of the train. He had timed it perfectly, for just as he finished selling in the last coach of all the train drew into the terminus platform. The journey had taken forty minutes; he had given eight little addresses of two minutes each, and he had sold thirty-nine Gospels. It was forty minutes well spent, with witness-bearing and Scripture selling intermingled. In eight coaches he had given a Gospel message, aroused some interest and sold some Scriptures.

Work of that kind is physically exacting and puts a severe strain on the throat. As a rule he does it only one day a week, except at Easter and Christmas when he does it for six days in succession, and has hardly any voice left when the week comes to an end. 'But it is worth it', he says with a smile, 'for I sell a lot of Scriptures and have many talks with people.

Last Good Friday I sold 537 Gospels in that one day, and more than 1,000 in the week.' On other days he goes from house to house or works along cinema queues. He concentrates on the great seasons of the Christian year, and uses the familiar Roman Catholic phrases such as 'the blessed Virgin Mary'. He does this deliberately for although great numbers of the people are not Christian believers and still greater numbers never enter a church, there is a certain Roman Catholic cultural background that is more or less familiar to every Brazilian. To the question whether people ever write to him in response to his invitation, or call at his home, he replied quite unequivocally. 'Yes', he said, 'they write sometimes, but more often they come to see me at my house. There are few Saturdays when I do not get any callers. I generally get about four or eight each Saturday, and they are nearly always genuine seekers. That gives me my chance and many of them become truly converted. I find out where they live and give them the address of the nearest Protestant church. I know that at least some of them join up.'

Such is the method adopted by that particular colporteur who works in a Brazilian city where there are suburban trains and cinema queues. A colporteur in Cyprus, where these features are not found, must necessarily follow a different practice. His approach must be more leisurely than is possible in the few minutes between stations on a suburban train. He must spend time with people. He must visit lonely cottages scattered over the countryside and must drop in at the coffee shops where the people spend their leisure time, especially in the evenings, talking, drinking coffee and playing cards. The colporteur takes advantage of the fact that when they are there they are in leisured mood, ready not only to talk but also to listen and to look. He accordingly sits down amongst them and joins in their conversation. If it is a Moslem village, made up of people of Turkish descent, he adjusts his conversation accordingly. After a time he opens his bag, saying, 'I've got some interesting books here. They tell how the world was made and how plants and animals and man came to be. They are just the kind of books you will like to read. Here they are. Have a look at them for yourselves.' And he brings out half a dozen Scripture portions, attractively produced with cover designs in the Turkish style. Since it is a Moslem village he does not bring out St. Mark's Gospel, because its opening words about 'Jesus Christ the Son of God' are likely to give offence to people who emphatically deny that God had a Son. He hands the copies round and encourages the men to read them for themselves. Some turn over the pages eagerly, others in the fumbling fashion of those who are unaccustomed to handling books. One man opens the book and then looks up and says, 'But these are Christian books. We are Moslems here and do not want them.' To which the colporteur replies by reminding them that the Holy Koran speaks about Abraham and Moses and David and Jesus and others, and that these books tell the story of these great ones. To prove it he picks up a copy of Genesis and reads an extract or two about Abraham and Jacob. He may then pick up a Gospel and read one of the parables. Another villager breaks in and says that the books are no good to him because he cannot read; which leads the colporteur to say that surely his children can read and suggests that one of them should read the little book to him. Yet another man says that he can't afford to buy because the price is too high, to which the colporteur replies that he will let him have a copy at half-price or even less if he will promise to read it. So the talk goes on, with a good deal of genial country humour inter-mingled with this conversational give and take. The col-porteur appreciates this, for he knows how important it is for his work to have an atmosphere of friendliness and good-will. Occasionally he is met with frowns and disapproval, and he quickly realises that he must not be too pushful with his books. By friendliness and persistence, however, he generally manages to sell a few portions and to make a few contacts which he will follow up on some subsequent occasion. Care and tact are always needed in Moslem areas, for a thoughtless word may at any moment cause a flare-up of fanaticism. The colporteur knows that results come slowly in a Moslem country. His usual method is therefore to sell a portion of Scripture and establish a friendly relationship with the purchaser, so that on subsequent visits to the area, he will quite naturally pay him a friendly call, in the course of which he will ask how the reading is going, and will encourage its continuance. That may not seem to be much, and for some time he may have to content himself with that. He will need patience and he will have to trust that the book will make its own impression and perhaps one day the purchaser will, of his own accord, begin to ask for information and even seek instruction. Difficult though it may be to win a convert from Islam, experience shows that there is nothing better for the purpose than a copy of the Bible. No one knew this better than Dr. Samuel Zwemer who gave a lifetime of service to work amongst Moslems, and who maintained that there was no tool half as useful as the Bible. While Dr. Christy Wilson, an acknowledged authority, wrote in *The Moslem World* that he had been 'surprised to find how many converts from Islam attribute their conversion to passages from the Old Testament'.[1]

A third and quite different method of using the Bible with an evangelistic purpose is one that has been widely adopted in Japan. The pastor of a church works out a plan for reaching

[1] Christy Wilson in *The Moslem World*, July 1937, p. 237.

every home in a near-by village or in a new suburb that is
growing up on the fringe of the city where he lives. He
secures the promise of ten or a dozen young men in his church
to give perhaps half a day each week to helping him with
Scripture distribution. They start out with large parcels of
Scriptures strapped on the backs of their bicycles, while the
pastor carries on his machine a portable projector, a screen
and a few films. On arriving at their destination they visit
every house in the area. They have previously had some
guidance in the art of bookselling, and they find little diffi-
culty in getting rid of their books and pamphlets. Few
countries in the world have so large a proportion of literate
people as Japan, and books are always welcome. But the
pastor is not content with selling portions of Scripture.
He wants to set the claims of Christ before the people; so he
instructs his team of helpers to tell all those who buy a
portion two things—first, that the book they have bought
is the most precious book in the world, and second, that
if they will bring their portion with them they will be
admitted free of charge to a film-showing that is to take
place as soon as it is dark. This invitation ensures not only a
full house, but also that people come in an expectant attitude
of mind. The films are specially chosen and lead up to one
that deals with the life of Christ and has a strong evangelistic
appeal.

In each of these cases the Bible is being used with a view
to evangelism. The Brazilian colporteur selling Gospels on a
suburban train gives a Gospel message and follows it up with
a personal talk with any who care to call at his home. The
Cypriot colporteur calling at Turkish coffee shops goes on
year after year cultivating the friendship of those who buy
his books, in the hope that one day they will openly
acknowledge the claims of Christ. The Japanese pastor with

his team of helpers selling books from door to door, presses home the message by showing films of the life of Christ. In each case what is done has an evangelistic purpose; and in each case those who are engaged in this evangelistic work are Bible distributors. They are in fact colporteurs of one kind or another.

Scripture distribution by colporteurs is not some new device just lately adopted. It has been in use nearly as long as the Bible societies have been in existence. The essence of colportage is that a man with a Bible in his hand confronts a man who does not possess one, and tries to persuade him to buy one or accept it as a gift; and he does so not primarily to sell a book, but because he believes that the book contains God's message to men. His purpose is fundamentally evangelistic. His bookselling is his method of evangelism. For along with every copy of the Scriptures that he sells there goes a conversation or a personal Christian witness. He is thus something more than a bookseller; he is also an evangelist; and if he is good at his job he will take care that his interest in bookselling does not obscure his zeal for evangelism. Indeed, the purpose of this part of the book is to show that colportage is a form of evangelism, and the colporteur a front-line evangelist, and also that the Bible is the colporteur's best evangelistic tool.

In all that follows it should be borne in mind that a colporteur is not necessarily a full-time, paid agent. He may be a part-time worker; he may be entirely voluntary; he may be a pastor who promotes Bible distribution throughout his parish; or he may be a layman who carries a couple of portions in his pocket to give to someone as he may have opportunity. He is essentially an individual worker, whether he goes off alone on a long tour of remote hamlets, or whether he stands by a bookstall in an Eastern market, or whether he makes a contact with a fellow-guest in an hotel. His approach is personal and individual.

The first mark of a good colporteur or distributor of the Scriptures, whether he is full-time or part-time, paid or voluntary, is that he is ready to give time to people. He does not just try to sell a book and then pass on. He sits down and talks and gradually leads the conversation round to the book and its message. He makes no attempt to distribute his books wholesale; he disposes of them one by one. Every book he sells means that he has spoken a word to someone and has made a Christian contact. Though he sells books, he is more than a bookseller; he is a special kind of unofficial evangelist, one who always has a book in his hand, and one who knows the book through and through, and can quote it from memory or turn to a passage and read it without a moment's hesitation. His sphere is the wayside, the market-place, the street door and the village inn. He is the apostle of casual contacts, turning a bus-ride or a wait in a railway station to account. He is a familiar figure in town and country from China to Peru. He drops in at the Japanese tea-shop, he chats in the Mexican town square, he calls at the lonely farmhouse in Canada or Finland, he is known in the Indian village and the Scottish clachan. Everywhere he goes he sells Scriptures and makes the gospel known. 'There have been two conversions this month', writes a colporteur in Iran, a notoriously difficult field for evangelistic work. 'I met them in the street and sold them Scriptures. They started to read them at once, and at a later date they came back to me and confessed their faith in Christ. They have since been put in touch with a church.' An experience of this kind is not uncommon and again and again the colporteur proves himself a front-line evangelist. 'The Gospel portions that I sell', writes a colporteur in Burma, 'are bought and read by people who know nothing about Christ. They are, however, willing to read and find out. Just recently two men who bought Bibles from me have come to believe in Christ through their reading, and have now been baptised.'[1] Another colporteur, this time in Peru, tells of 'families to whom he had sold Scriptures in eight different villages who have been brought into the Christian fellowship through reading the Word of God'.[2] In hundreds of cases such as these the colporteur is bookseller and evangelist rolled into one.

A second mark of a good colporteur is that he is a pioneer and frontiersman. He stands at the place where Christian and non-Christian meet. In many cases he is the first to introduce the Christian message, and in that sense he is a real pioneer evangelist. In Cyprus the present writer travelled with a colporteur, who a few months previously had sheltered from a storm in a Moslem home. He was invited by his host to tell the other guests what his books were about. 'I explained that they were Christian books, and I read some extracts from Job and the Sermon on the Mount. "But this", they exclaimed, "is a good book and its words are sweet. Why do the sheiks tell us that Christian books teach belief in many gods?" I replied that we Christians believe that God is one and has no partner or equal in majesty.' There were further explanations and in the end the host bought a Bible and several of the others took Gospels. Never before had any of them seen a Bible or heard it read. Times out of number the colporteur is the first to make the Christian message known. 'We are just back', writes the leader of a colportage team in Brazil, 'from Porocatu, a new place which is being opened up. We visited every house, every hut, every palm-leaf tent. For many people it was the first time anyone had ever spoken to them about the gospel.'[3]

[1] *The Bible in the World*, March–April 1952, p. 31.

[2] C. W. Turner, *La Biblia en America Latina*, p. 38.   [3] *Ibid.*, p. 34.

There are occasions when the results are more spectacular than the two just given; when converts come not in ones and twos, but in scores and even hundreds. Some years ago in the Haute Vienne area in France, the whole district was so stirred by the visits of a number of colporteurs that evangelists and pastors had to be called in to gather the harvest into the church. In Belgium the position is even more striking, for there evangelical Christianity is said to owe its very existence to Bible society colporteurs. The same is true in the mission field where case after case can be quoted of indigenous churches that are the fruit of some colporteur's visit or that had their origin in some Gospel or New Testament left by a passer-by years before. A church that had an origin of this kind was found by a colporteur in a rural district in Brazil a few years ago. He had been in the neighbourhood some years before and had sold a Bible to a farmer. The farmer took it home and started to read it, but because his wife objected, he gave it up. After a time, however, she changed her mind and they agreed to read it together. Before long they realised that they could not keep it to themselves, and they asked another couple to join them. The four had to put up with a good deal of petty persecution, but they persisted and one by one others joined them, and when the colporteur paid his second visit he found 120 people gathered for worship. A somewhat similar story comes from one of the more remote parts of Peru where a farmer and his wife, somewhere about 1890, secured a Bible from a passing colporteur and started Bible reading and family worship. Others joined them, including many of the men working on the farm. Word was sent to a missionary in the capital, who paid a number of visits and eventually formed the little company into a Christian congregation. There followed, for some reason, a period of neglect and for forty years not a single visit was paid. But the little church continued, nurturing its life during the whole of that time solely on the Bible. In 1937 the visits were resumed and the community began to blossom out and is now the centre of a group of thriving churches.

A third mark of a good colporteur is that he seeks contacts with homes. The two instances just given are cases in point. He believes that in order to plant the Christian cause firmly in any area the best thing he can do is to get the Bible into the home. He holds, as St. Chrysostom held long ago, that the battle is half won when a Bible has its place in the home. This sense of the strategic importance of homes has led him to adopt the practice of going from door to door with his books. For more than a hundred years colporteurs have followed this practice and they are still following it fruitfully, both in the mission field and in the home countries. An informal enquiry made in 1947 showed that in a good many parts of the world it is still the most successful way of distributing the Scriptures. During recent years, however, the method has come in for some criticism, and is being used rather less than formerly in the towns and cities of the West, although it shows no signs of falling off in the rural areas. In the case of small scattered communities, it is almost the only way of ensuring that the Bible is brought to the attention of every family. The Bible may, of course, be sent through the post to every home, but then there is no personal contact; and experience proves that it is the personal contact that counts. Whatever may be said in criticism of the door-to-door method, it is still—for many parts of the world—the best means of selling the Scriptures and commending the faith. F. C. Glass, speaking out of fifty years' experience in both town and country in Brazil, affirms that the house-to-house method is still the best. 'It is,' he says, 'more systematic, more personal, more fruitful and more satisfying than any other. In the market people come and go; they may leave in the middle of a sentence and stroll away or go off to their business. At the house door there is more leisure, and more chance of fruitful personal contact. What is more, you can go back to the same door the next day or the next week.'

As every colporteur knows, the method calls for a good deal of tact and persistence, but it pays in the end. A Canadian colporteur called upon a Ukrainian family that had recently settled in Saskatchewan. 'When I first called the husband kept rejecting the Bible I offered. There were many excuses, no money, no time, no interest. But I countered by saying that those were vain excuses. At long last he accepted a Ukrainian Bible, saying: "Perhaps my wife will pay you with chickens when she comes home; if not, she will give the Bible back." Some weeks later I returned for payment. The parents were not at home, but the children were. They told me that both father and mother were reading the Bible every evening. Said the seventeen-year-old son, "I think they must have read it through already." And the fifteen-year-old daughter added: "Yes, and Dad is telling us what the Bible teaches and what we should do." '[1]

A wise colporteur, who looks for permanent results from his work, is not content merely to sell Scriptures from door to door. He tries to link new Bible readers to some local church if there is one, or with other Bible readers when there is no worshipping group within reach. The colporteur knows that fellowship is essential to the Christian life, especially to isolated Bible readers living in a non-Christian setting. A colporteur in pre-communist China had for years been in the habit of going from shop to shop and house to house. But he was often disappointed because many of his new Bible

[1] Mildred Cable and Francesca French, *The Spark and the Flame*, p. 85.

readers lost their zeal, until he hit upon the plan of putting them in touch with one another and forming them into a worshipping group which in time became a duly organised church.

A fourth mark of a good colporteur is that he goes where the people are. He goes from market to market and festival to festival. He is always on the move, travelling in all kinds of ways, on foot and bicycle, by bullock-cart and bus, by camel and motor-car, by boat and train, by mule and even by aeroplane. Sometimes his equipment is only a satchel or a pair of panniers over a pony's back, sometimes it is a folding table or even a motor-van that can become bookstall, pulpit or bedroom as required. For the most part his equipment is a small case in which he carries as complete a selection of Scriptures as he can manage. As he packs his bag he has the non-Christian mainly in view, and that means that he takes Gospels and Testaments rather than whole Bibles. He plans primarily for the non-Christian, because he knows that his proper place is where evangelism is to be done. He accordingly sets up his stall where the people are: in markets and fairs, at pagan assemblies and places of pilgrimage, in railway stations and city squares; wherever, in fact, the crowds gather. One man sets up his stall near the bathing ghats in Benares, where the pilgrim-multitudes come and go, while his colleague mingles with the pilgrims in the crowded streets. Almost every book that they sell is taken back to a Hindu home. What the result is no one knows, save that now and then a word is received showing that the seed fell in good soil. Another man, in this case a theological student who takes his turn with other students from the same college in Calcutta, sits on the pavement outside the college gate with a selection of Scriptures beside him and chats with passers-by and sells a few books. Yet another man adopts a somewhat different technique. He finds a convenient spot in a village market where he squats on the ground with his parcel of books open before him. He draws attention to his wares and invites enquiry. It may be that most of those who stand around cannot read, but he can generally find someone, a boy perhaps, who is ready to read a few passages aloud. The villagers listen, and presently one produces a coin and then another, and off they go each with a Scripture portion which is read aloud that evening, perhaps for the first time, in a non-Christian home. Yet another man makes a point of going to towns on their market days or fêtes. He takes his place at a point where people are accustomed to gather round and talk. He sets up his stall and arranges his books; he talks to any who come, he explains why he is there and says what his books are about; he picks up one and reads a short section. Sometimes he gives a brief address; and occasionally he has a few friends who sing; but more often he just chats with all and sundry and brings the conversation round to his books and their message. Occasionally he is jeered at or even manhandled and his books are sometimes thrown about or destroyed; but generally he is not interfered with, especially if he is good-tempered and courteous. Still another man keeps on the move, pushing a cycle-trolley, with books fastened to the tops and sides, stopping here and there wherever he finds a likely-looking group. In Burma, before the war, a man used to travel up and down the road to Mandalay with a bookshelf lashed to the back of his car, selling books—to use his own words—'in unprecedented numbers'. In Brazil, a motor launch, with two colporteurs on board, goes up and down the great rivers, visiting towns and villages hardly accessible otherwise. In a dozen countries, book vans are in use, perhaps visiting remote hamlets in Pakistan or tiny kraals on the South African karroo, or sun-scorched villages in the sandy stretches of Tunisia. As many men, so many methods. But though the methods differ, the purpose remains the same; namely, to sell the Book and introduce the faith. How far the methods are successful is shown to some extent by the statistics of Scriptures sold and converts won, and to some extent by the enquiries that follow a visit, and even by such testimonials as that which appeared not so long ago in a Mohammedan paper called *The Moslem Censor*, which said: 'The trouble with these books (i.e. the Christian Scriptures) is not in any special passage, but that everyone who reads them wants to become a Christian.'

A more detailed illustration, this time from the Central American Republic of El Salvador, may not be out of place here, especially as the colporteur in question has worked out a fruitful technique of his own. He has found from experience that it takes practically as much time, effort and persuasion to sell a packet of ten or a dozen portions as it takes to sell a single one. He accordingly makes up little parcels of the Gospels, Acts, Romans, Proverbs, some thirteen booklets in all, arranged with their bright covers outwards, and wraps each parcel in cellophane. With a bag-full of these packets and a handful of illustrated 'St. Luke' in magazine format, he goes to the market when it is full of people and buzzing with talk. He goes up to a stall where two or three people are standing and shows them the illustrated Luke. As he turns over the pages and shows the pictures he soon has their attention. He goes on to explain the pictures and to tell their story. Now and again he reads a few paragraphs that bear on the pictures, and he adds something about the Christian message. When he thinks the interest of his listeners is sufficiently aroused, he will point out that what is said briefly in the illustrated volume is set out in more detail in the packet of little booklets and that the whole set, including the illustrated one, costs only a few centavos. The response, of course, will vary. Sometimes there will be an immediate request for a packet, and that will generally be followed by others, especially if the first buyer is the kind of person whose example others are inclined to follow. Sometimes a man will say that he is not interested and does not want to buy. A statement of that kind will often dissuade others who might be on the point of buying. This particular colporteur tries to avoid a situation of this kind by concentrating on someone of his listeners whose interest he thinks he can secure and whose lead others are likely to follow. In this way he not only secures sales, but he also forestalls discouraging statements. The present writer has watched this particular colporteur at work both in town and country. He has watched the faces of the people, noted their reactions, recorded the time taken to sell a packet and worked out the average time needed to effect a sale in the city and also in the country. As might be expected sales take place rather more quickly in the city market where people are accustomed to making more rapid decisions, than in a country market where everything moves at a more leisurely pace. In the city the time required to effect a sale worked out at an average of three minutes and two seconds; in the country at five minutes and three seconds. Moreover each sale meant that fourteen booklets were disposed of; and experience showed that in nearly every case the purchaser of a packet distributed the contents to relatives and neighbours. One sale thus meant about a dozen readers and an obvious enlargement of the evangelistic appeal.

It has already been said that the term colporteur is here used to indicate not only the full-time, paid agent, but also the part-time, voluntary worker, and indeed any Christian man or woman who takes an occasional share in distributing a few copies of the Scriptures. These voluntary and occasional helpers should also have the same marks. As far as possible they should give time to individuals, should try to reach the outsider, should get in touch with homes, and should go where the people are. They will have to make the necessary modifications in method, but in essence the four 'marks' will still be necessary. This needs to be stressed in view of the fact that Scripture distribution must become more and more a function of the Church and of the church member.

In country after country the colporteur is the front-line representative of the Christian cause, and is often the first to make contact with the non-Christian. In some places he is almost the only one who is even attempting to do so. And the Bible is his constant companion. 'I've got some books here', says a colporteur who has been chatting with a group of men in a Mexican inn. 'I know that as educated people you are interested in books, and I am sure you will be interested in these. Here is one that has some first-rate poetry in it, and here's another that contains some very remarkable stories. Let me read you one or two bits so that you can judge for yourselves.' And he reads a psalm and follows it with one of the parables. With the Bible in his hand the colporteur is ready and equipped; he can talk about the Christian message and can do so effectively. Without it he feels himself at sea. 'One day I set out for the railway station', writes a Siamese colporteur-evangelist. 'I was intending to preach there, but I forgot to take my books with me. When I got to my destination I did not know what to do or how to begin. On the following day I took some Scripture portions to sell and tracts to distribute. This time I preached without ceasing and messages came to me in abundance.'[1]

The Bible is the colporteur's talking-point. It provides him with a text both for selling his books and for commending his message. It is his constant companion and of necessity he

[1] *American Bible Society Report*, 1952, p. 279.

knows it through and through. 'I make a practice of carrying a marked copy of a Gospel in my pocket', says a layman who has done a great deal both of Scripture distribution and of personal evangelism. 'I give it to the man sitting opposite me in the train or to the man I meet in the hotel. I say to him: "I have read this little book with great interest, especially the parts I have marked. I should like you to read it too."' 'I always take a Bible with me', writes an experienced evangelist, 'especially when I am going to see people whom I have not previously met. It is my visiting card as well as my best friend.' The two men just quoted are not colporteurs or Bible workers; but in their Christian work they have learnt how important it is to have a Bible or a Gospel at hand when they want to confront a man with the claims of Christ.

No other book can compare with it as a means of bringing individuals to a definite decision. No other book would ever be quoted to a seeker in an enquiry room; nor would any other book be read or quoted to a Chicago gangster or a confirmed drunkard who was seeking to make a fresh start. Personal conversation and counselling and prayer may bring a man to a receptive frame of mind; they may even bring him to the point of saying, 'Almost thou persuadest me to be a Christian'. But in a great number of cases something more is needed. Bunyan describes that something more when he says in his *Pilgrim's Progress* that he 'dreamed a dream and saw a man clothed in rags, standing in a certain place, with his face from his own house, a book in his hand, and a burden upon his back. . . . And he did open the book and read therein.' It was the reading that mattered, for after reading the Book Bunyan says that he went up to the cross and 'his burden loosed from his shoulders and fell from off his back'. The timely use of the Scriptures plays an important part in personal evangelism. Many an interview has had no result just because the Bible was not used or was used blunderingly. On the other hand, countless interviews have borne rich fruit because the Bible itself or its quoted words were used at the right moment and in the right way. In Bunyan's dream he saw that at a certain point the man 'did open the book and read therein'. There is a point, so most experienced workers agree, when the enquirer should be encouraged to listen to the words of Scripture or read them for himself. When conversation, prayer and friendship have done all they can to prepare the way, it is well to let the Bible have its chance. Scripture reading, coming as a climax, is more likely than anything else to lead the way to decision. Some of the clearest evidence of this is found in some of the most unexpected places.

Rarely has the place of the Bible in evangelism been more unmistakably demonstrated than in the work of human reclamation that is carried on in one of the world's most notorious districts. Skidrow, in the heart of the 'Loop' area in Chicago, is the home of gangsters, toughs, drunks, prostitutes and narcotics. In this unsavoury underworld of drink-shops, brothels, gambling dens and pawnshops, a number of Christian organisations are at work, among them the Harbour Light (Salvation Army), the Pacific Garden and the Christian Industrial League. One of them has been there for over twenty-five years, another for over forty, and the third for over seventy-five years. Between them they have accumulated a fund of experience that can hardly be equalled and probably nowhere surpassed. All of them deal with the same kind of people; all of them adopt pretty much the same methods; all of them use the Bible as their regular tool; and all of them can point to the same kind of results. The leader of the Harbour Mission, who was himself once listed by the police as an 'incurable', has had a hand in the conversion and rehabilitation of some 5,000 Skidrow 'toughs'. The Pacific

Garden Mission reports that it knows of over 50,000 converts since its work was started; while the Christian Industrial League reports that in the last twenty-one years they have had 84,000 conversions, or an average of 4,000 a year. Allowing for the probability that many—perhaps even the majority—of these conversions are not permanent, it means that thousands of Chicago's most abandoned and incorrigible inhabitants are steadily being changed into good Christians and law-abiding citizens. It is one of the miracles of the day.

The question is how these results are achieved. The answer is simple. The three organisations adopt much the same methods. A meal, a bath and a bed are always available. Personal counselling goes on all through the day and part of the night, and it is in these talks that the workers, often ex-drunks themselves, come to grips with individuals. They do not argue; they quote the Bible, or perhaps they read a verse or two. Experience has taught them that there is nothing so effective as the words of Scripture. The following extract from a report of one of the missions is fairly typical. A man who has come to the end of his tether, and is sitting alone with one of the workers, keeps on saying: 'I'm such a punk that Jesus can't save me. No one can.' He bursts into tears. The worker takes him by the arm and says, 'Listen to this. Him that cometh unto me I will in no wise cast out.' 'What does that say?' asks the man. The worker reads it again and adds: 'Do you think He will cast you out?' 'I hope not', replies the man. 'What do you mean—you hope not? You can be sure. Listen to this.' Then he reads the verse again, and goes through the whole conversation once more until both the words and their meaning are firmly lodged in the man's mind. In a few minutes he is on his feet. His maudlin tears are gone. There is firmness and confidence in his voice as he says, 'Yes, I know He's my Saviour. He's saved even me.'[1] The workers in the Pacific Garden Mission say that in ninety per cent. of the conversions of which they have record the operative factor is the Bible. In the Harbour Light Mission their practice in their personal counselling work is to put a New Testament or a booklet of Bible extracts into the man's hands and they ask him to read one or two specified verses aloud, so that the man himself reads the Bible's answer to his need. They know that the words will have an effect that their own words will not. The leader of the Christian Industrial League says that in their work they have found that St. John's Gospel is the best for dealing with these tough, hard men. Its straight, unequivocal words about sin and salvation somehow go home and carry conviction to the most abandoned, while its direct invitation wins a response that nothing else does. An enquiry extending over five years, made by the leader of the mission amongst the men themselves, showed that the verse which had more influence with them than any other was 'Come unto me all ye that labour and are heavy laden and I will give you rest'. The same mission has also found that if any worker, during an interview, does most of the talking himself, or tries to argue, or pushes his own notions or Scriptural hobby-horse, he gets very little response. If he attempts to 'explain prophecy' or to 'interpret Daniel' the result is that he distracts attention and defeats his purpose. It is the words of the Bible 'without note or comment' which go deepest and carry most conviction. The practice in this mission is for the worker to give to the visitor at the end of an interview a little folder entitled 'Put in Your Name'. It consists of five brief passages, such as 'God so loved the world that he gave his only-begotten Son that . . . . should not perish but have everlasting life'. The enquirer is invited to write his name where the dots appear in each of the five quotations, thus clinching his decision and building it on God's Word revealed in the Scriptures. All this is evidence of the first importance for those who are concerned with the place of the Bible in evangelism, especially since it relates to some of the world's most abandoned men.

To pass from this reclamation work in Chicago's underworld to the evangelistic fervour of one of Dr. Billy Graham's organised missions is not as different as might be supposed. Dr. Graham makes no attempt at swaying the crowd with oratory or appealing to the emotions; he relies almost entirely on driving home the message of the Bible. A kind of refrain in all his addresses is 'The Bible says . . . the Bible says. . . .' He expounds it and thrusts its message home with tremendous urgency. But however much he relies on the Bible in his sermons, he trusts to it even more in the work that his helpers do after his address is over. 'We have learned', he says, 'that it takes about five per cent. effort to win a man to Christ and ninety-five per cent. to keep him in Christ and growing into maturity in the Church.'[1] In order to try and 'keep' converts, he has a large group of 'counsellors' who have been carefully trained to deal with enquirers. Their training is almost entirely biblical. They have to memorize a fairly wide range of passages and be able to quote them or turn to them at a moment's notice. This study of the Bible is turned to account in the enquiry room, where each counsellor is given the care of one of the enquirers, with a view to leading the enquirer to a clear Christian decision based on the objective, written Word of God. The counsellor quotes some of the great promises of the Bible, and helps the enquirer to apply them to himself. He turns to the actual passages and reads them slowly and with care so that their significance may sink in. Finally he gives the

[1] Billy Graham *The Work of an Evangelist*, p. 19.

enquirer a copy of St. John's Gospel and a little booklet, entitled *Initial Bible Rations*, made up mainly of Bible passages arranged under suitable headings for a new convert to learn and ponder. One of Graham's colleagues expressed the opinion that it is the biblical follow-up in the enquiry room itself and subsequently, that is the secret of Graham's success. 'Instead of losing ninety per cent. of the converts', he said, 'we keep ninety per cent. of them.' Graham's method thus seems to be the use of the Bible first, last and all the time. The preparation of the counsellors consists mainly of Bible study with a view to its evangelistic use, especially in the enquiry room; Graham's own message from the pulpit or platform is urgent biblical preaching; while the follow-up with the enquirers consists very largely of getting them to read or learn suitable Bible passages. It is not enough that they should obtain a Bible; buying one is not being converted; they must read it and study it and make its message their own. Here again is evidence that is important for the present purpose, in that it shows the part that the Bible can play in large-scale mass evangelism and especially in the personal counselling of individual enquirers that goes with it.

Various ways of using the Bible in personal contacts with individual men and women have been reviewed in this chapter. It has been demonstrated that the Bible can be used fruitfully with people of almost every kind, whether they are busy city folk in a suburban train, or peasants at their leisure in a village coffee shop, or American toughs from the Chicago underworld. When wisely used the Bible can obviously speak to every man's condition, whatever that condition may be. Success or failure seems to depend not on the book, but on the man who uses it and on the methods he adopts. One of the factors of success seems to be to use the actual words of Scripture as much as possible. Not to argue; not to try to build up a convincing case; but to let the Bible speak, either by quoting it from memory or by producing a copy and reading a passage, or by encouraging the listener to read the passage for himself. The actual production of the physical book, so that it can be seen and handled and its very words read, seems to be one of the most efficacious methods. Some workers prefer not to produce the book itself, at least not until the interview is well advanced, but to quote appropriate passages from memory. The majority, however, prefer to have the book in their hands. It seems to give concreteness and objectivity to the words and also to create confidence in the enquirer.

Another factor to be commended is to take time with people. Whether it is at the house door or in the village inn, at the market stall or in the enquiry room, what matters, particularly from an evangelistic point of view, is to be un-hurried. A quick sale may not really awaken interest, and if interest is not aroused the chances are that the book will be put aside and forgotten. If the colporteur is to have the assur-ance that the book will be read, and especially that it will be read with an expectant and eager mind, he must first of all arouse sufficient interest. He must therefore be unhurried in his contacts and must take enough time not merely to sell a man a book, but to kindle his interest sufficiently to make him keen to read what he has bought.

A third factor to be commended, from the point of view of evangelism, is to link the new reader to other Scripture readers, and if possible to a worshipping community of Christian people, so that from the first he will be not a lone reader liable to give up, but a member of a fellowship of readers. It is for this reason important that the colporteur should work in as close co-operation as possible with the Church, so that he may link the new buyers of the Scriptures and the new readers to the community of Christ's people.

VI

USING THE BIBLE IN
CONCERTED EFFORTS

THIS CHAPTER will be concerned with the way in which
the Scriptures are used in special concerted efforts in the field
of evangelism today, whether they are organised by a single
denomination or mission, or whether they are joint enterprises in which the various churches or missions of an area
take part. Evidence will be brought first of all from Latin
America, then from Africa and Asia, then from North
America and the European continent. This will be followed
by some discussion of such special ventures as the widespread
free distribution of the Scriptures, the use of audio-visual aids,
and the growth of Bible correspondence courses. In all these
varying types of evangelistic activity the Bible is seen to be
a valued and an effective tool.

1. *In Latin America*

It is often said that the Christian Church is growing most
rapidly in precisely those places where the Bible is being
distributed most eagerly. However true this may be of
other parts of the world, it is certainly true of Brazil,
where evangelical Christianity is said, on good authority,[1]
to be growing more rapidly than anywhere else on earth.
Not only are there strong churches and large congregations,
but there are also large numbers of people waiting to be
admitted to church membership. The Presbyterians are said
to be growing so rapidly that they cannot keep pace with

[1] J. Merle Davis, *How the Church Grows in Brazil*, p. 72.

those who are seeking admission to the church. They have at least twice as many enquirers as they have full communicant members. The Methodists are said to be growing with equal speed. While it is common knowledge that the Pentecostals and the Baptists are growing most rapidly of all! When the question is raised of the reason for this phenomenal growth, one of the answers always given is that the Bible has a good deal to do with it. Some church leaders think that it is one of the chief causes. The Secretary of the Bible Society of Brazil, for example, commenting on this in his report for 1952, asks 'How account for the vitality, the strength, the progress, the dreams, the influence of the evangelical movement in Brazil? The answer is: it is Bible-centred. Evangelical Brazilians believe in the Bible.'[1] He goes on to quote the opinion of a visitor with wide experience of Christian work in many parts of the world, who wrote, 'In my many travels I have never encountered a people so Bible-conscious as the evangelical people of Brazil'.

The most rapidly growing denomination (with the possible exception of the Pentecostals, whose precise figures are not easy to obtain) is the Baptist. In spite of rather strict standards of admission, they are adding to their numbers every day. They have always laid great stress on evangelism as a permanent function of the church, but for the last ten years they have gone further and adopted the practice of observing the month of September as a special month of evangelism. They focus all their energies, in prayer, in planning and in action, upon this month, making it a kind of annual ingathering or harvest. They follow a recognised plan according to which the first week of the month is devoted to prayer and preparation; the second to a systematic visitation of every house in the community, when a copy of St. John's Gospel

[1] Ewaldo Alves, in *American Bible Society Report*, 1952, p. 231.

is given to every family, and a word of Christian witness added, together with an invitation to the meetings of the following week; the third week is the mission itself with meetings of many kinds; and the fourth is devoted to visiting the homes of those who, during the previous week, signed a decision card, entered an enquiry room, asked for further information, or gave any other indication of special interest. At this second visitation the enquirer is given another Gospel to read, together with the first of a series of small tracts on the meaning of the Christian faith.

It is obvious that in a concerted effort of this kind evangelism and the Scriptures are so closely interwoven that it is practically impossible to disentangle them. The Bible is an essential part of the total effort. What is more, this kind of evangelism has proved itself to be abundantly fruitful, and is regarded by the Brazilian Baptists themselves as the main reason for their phenomenal growth. They use nearly a third of a million Scriptures, mostly copies of St. John's Gospel, every year; and they could use many more if more were available. They do not give them away; they sell them; and they sell a large proportion of them during the annual house-to-house visitation already referred to. No church in Brazil uses the Scriptures more consistently and none grows more rapidly.

This feature of the close association of Bible distribution with church expansion can be illustrated, though somewhat less dramatically, from other parts of Latin America as different as Argentina, Chile, Costa Rica, Mexico and Cuba. In Argentina there is no feature of the Church's life that more impresses the visitor from Europe. One of the largest Protestant communions in the country has adopted as its slogan, 'Let us Sow'. Ministers, laymen, women and young people throughout the country have bent their energies to the task.

Half a dozen other Protestant communions in the country have launched somewhat similar campaigns. The results of this widespread activity have been truly impressive. And in the forefront of it all has been the Bible. 'In all their endeavours', writes the Bible Society secretary in Argentina,[1] 'these groups have leaned heavily on the Bible Society for the provision of the indispensable Scriptures and for advice concerning distribution. From different parts of the country many expressions of gratitude have come for the help that the Bible has been in the endeavour to reach the outsider. In this spirit a pastor recently wrote, "We were enabled through your help to carry out our wish to combine the distribution of the Scriptures with our campaign of special meetings"; and another said that "Through the co-operation of the Bible Society, it has been possible to intensify our evangelistic effort by sending a copy of the New Testament to a large number of selected people".'

In Chile, too, the Bible has come alive and mainly in association with active evangelism. For some years the circulation of the Bible has been growing step-by-step with the growing evangelistic activity of the Church. Recent developments, however, have surpassed anything previously known. On the one hand there has been a well-planned and almost nation-wide evangelistic campaign, which has made a profound impression, and on the other hand there has been an increase in Bible distribution that has broken all records. Once again evangelism and the circulation of the Scriptures have advanced together.

Turning to Central America, Costa Rica provides an excellent example of the way in which evangelism and the Scriptures can be linked in a special concerted effort. In 1952 the evangelical churches of San José carried through a united

[1] C. W. Turner, in *American Bible Society Report*, 1952, p. 210.

mission. They prepared for it by a house-to-house distribution of the Scriptures in the preceding weeks. The city was divided into areas and individual churches were asked to take responsibility for the visitation of certain streets. The visitors were chosen with care, instructed in methods of approach, equipped with Gospel portions and sent out two by two. In some cases they met with a rebuff, but on the whole they were well received as they went from door to door. They answered questions, bore their testimony, sold their books— more than 1,000 every day—and awakened interest in the forthcoming mission. Reviewing the mission a year later church leaders in the city agreed that the results were most encouraging where the workers were most carefully prepared. Some of the visitors had had only one hurried meeting for preparation, and they had gone to their task feeling nervous and ill-prepared. In some of these cases they lost heart and gave up when they were barely halfway through. Others, notably a group of theological students, had had a four-day course of instruction in approach and Bible-selling, and they had gone to their visitation confident and keen. They found that Gospel portions were excellent talking-points which enabled them to interest people in Christianity and in the forthcoming mission. Some of them continued their visitation long after the mission ended, helping individuals with their reading of the Scriptures, explaining their message and slowly winning them to the Christian side. In this particular effort the Bible was so closely tied in with the whole mission that it is hardly possible to speak of them separately. The Bible was an essential part of the mission, and the mission workers themselves declared that the Bible, more than anything else, enabled them to bring the message of God's grace home to the people of San José.

2. In Africa and Asia

Latin America, however, is not the only part of the world where the Bible and evangelism are closely linked. For a dozen years or more a revival has been taking place in Ruanda in the heart of the African continent, and has spread across the frontiers into Kenya, Uganda and Tanganyika. There can be no manner of doubt about either its reality or its connection with the Bible. 'In every place that the revival has touched', says Bishop Brazier, who has been closely associated with the revival movement, 'there has been a solid background of Bible teaching. . . . From its earliest days the African Church in Ruanda was solidly instructed in the Bible doctrines of salvation.'[1] It is not without significance that this Bible-based revival has been one of the sources of the fortitude that enabled many of the African Christians in Kenya to stand firm under the fiendish pressure of the Mau Mau movement.[2]

Perhaps the clearest evidence of all comes from South India and is linked with the name of Dr. Azariah, the late Bishop of Dornakal. He was not only himself a tireless evangelist, but he also made it clear that he expected every Christian man and woman to be an evangelist too. 'In the early Church', he said, 'it was the common man who spread the Gospel . . . from slave to slave, from soldier to soldier, from artisan to artisan.' And he hoped and prayed that he might see the same happen in India. He set the standard high and was keenly disappointed when his hopes were not realised. He was greatly troubled, for example, to find that in his own diocese only three-quarters of the Christians took any part in active evangelism. As he went from village to village the burden of his message was the need for evangelism. 'Has every believer here won another?' he would ask when the

[1] *World Dominion*, March–April 1951, p. 97.
[2] *Ibid.*, July–August 1953, p. 251.

Christians of the village were assembled. He would then lead them in a simple but impressive piece of ritual in which he also took part. To use his own words, he would tell the baptised members to place their hands on their heads and to repeat after him: 'I am a baptised Christian. Woe is me if I preach not the Gospel.'[1] It was something that the humblest villagers understood and that they did not forget. His other central concern was the spread of the Scriptures. He knew in his own personal experience how closely the study of the Bible was connected with the call to evangelism. 'My own life', he used to say,[2] 'has been revived and nourished mainly by two factors, perhaps by three. First, I put down the study of Holy Scripture. . . .'

Knowing this about him, it is not surprising to find that he organised annual evangelistic campaigns or Weeks of Witness, as they were often called. He shared in these demonstrations, walking side by side with simple village folk. He joined in the singing of Christian lyrics; he took part in the reading of sections from the Scriptures when the procession stopped at various points in the village street; and he shared in distributing Gospels to those who could read. In addition, he was always ready to give time to the laborious tasks of Bible translation and revision and of serving on committees for circulating the Scriptures. For him evangelism and the Bible were inseparably linked.

In Thailand, a country where Christianity has only a small following as yet, they have learned by experience that things really happen when evangelism and Bible distribution are carried on together. They accordingly concentrate on Bible study first of all and follow this up by organising the students into Gospel teams to do evangelistic work and sell Scripture portions. In one village recently a group of Christians

[1] Carol Graham, *Azariah of Dornakal*, p. 61.   [2] *Ibid.*, p. 18.

met every night for several weeks for Bible study. 'In that way', writes the Bible Society secretary in Thailand,[1] 'they began to understand the truth of the Gospel, which in turn gave them a real desire to share this truth with others. They decided not only to study the Word of God but to proclaim it to their neighbours in other villages. Now they go out regularly to witness and sell portions.' There have been results too: Scripture sales that have run into thousands, frequent requests for further information and occasionally baptisms as well.

These various campaigns, Weeks of Witness, village visits and other concerted efforts, have been primarily evangelistic in purpose, but they have all had the Bible as an invariable accompaniment. The evidence drawn from areas as different as Brazil, Costa Rica, India and Thailand, makes it clear that when the Bible is well-used the evangelistic results are outstanding. Those who share in the campaigns are convinced of the value of the Bible. They know from experience that it gives them the right starting-point and the best follow-up, while in innumerable cases, it clinches the argument for the individual and brings him to decision.

In addition to these campaigns that are primarily evangelistic in purpose, there are others, such as Bible weeks or months and Bible exhibitions, where the emphasis is on Bible distribution and Bible reading rather than evangelism. Here the main purpose is to draw attention to the Bible, particularly the attention of those who are rather outside the Church's life, in the hope that an interest in the Bible will be created which will prove to be a first step towards a closer identification with the Christian cause. The evangelistic purpose is present in these Bible campaigns but it does not obtrude itself.

[1] P. Volk, in *American Bible Society Report*, 1951, p. 264.

Bible campaigns and Bible weeks or months are usually organised on an area basis, perhaps that of a city or province, and the aim is to focus the attention of the whole community upon the Bible for a specified period. Such efforts are generally interdenominational in character and embrace all, or most of the local churches. Their success, in fact, depends to some extent on the completeness of the co-operation secured. In a Bible crusade recently organised in Peru,[1] the emphasis was laid on private visits rather than public meetings. A group of churches accepted responsibility for the crusade in a given area, which was then divided into sections and two church members were allocated to each section. The church members then started on a systematic visitation of every family, taking Scriptures and a few tracts with them. They kept a record of the families visited and the interest shown in each case. In this crusade the visitation was done by volunteers and was confined to visits to individual homes. A drive of this kind, though under the very different conditions of Indian village life, was organised some years ago throughout the diocese of Tinnevelly. This presented particular difficulties not only because most of the population live in scattered villages, but also because large numbers of the people cannot read and larger numbers are too poor to buy books. Yet as many as 12,000 Scriptures were sold and the impact made on the homes of the people was said to be considerable.[2] In the case of a Bible week or Bible month, the crusade usually takes the form of a unified effort in which all the churches and missions of an area attempt to influence not the individual families, but the community as a whole, and to do so not by private visits but by public meetings in halls,

[1] *The Bulletin* of the United Bible Societies, No. 3, p. 30.
[2] National Christian Council of India *Review*, May 1943.

schools, factories, churches and the open air. In this type of crusade, representatives of the churches generally join hands with the Bible societies. The whole effort is on a more elaborate and public scale than the house-visitation effort, and may include the use of films, pageants, plays and other audio-visual aids. Book-fairs, book-teas, Bible lectures and Bible demonstrations, Bible conferences and Bible camps have the same end in view, namely to call attention to the Bible and to induce people to buy it and read it.

Since Bible exhibitions have recently begun to come into fashion, a word should perhaps be added. Full-scale Bible exhibitions, requiring a large hall and a great deal of preparation, have in recent years been held in several cities in France, Belgium, Switzerland, Britain and elsewhere, and have generally attracted a good deal of attention. One section of the exhibition is generally devoted to the history of the Bible, showing reproductions of manuscripts or even actual Bibles of historic importance; another section deals with Bible translation, showing how it is carried out and exhibiting copies of translations into strange languages; yet another shows illustrated Bibles, Bibles for children, or Braille Bibles for the blind. Such exhibitions certainly draw attention to the Bible, and quite often they draw the attention of people who have previously had no interest in it. They are thus a means of breaking new ground and a particularly useful way of winning the interest of the 'intelligenzia'.

In general, it may be said that Bible campaigns, Bible weeks or Bible months and Bible exhibitions succeed in drawing people's attention to the Bible. The house visitations, public gatherings, displays and demonstrations that are part and parcel of these special efforts, bring the Bible to the notice of the general public in the area. They succeed also in securing good sales of Bibles, though this feature needs to be more fully developed. How far they have succeeded in winning new interest in the Christian cause is more difficult to say. All these campaigns are short-term ones, rarely going beyond a week or a month, while results in the form of lives changed or communities affected are not usually evident till much later. From an evangelistic point of view the important feature of these intensive crusades is that they aim by one method or another at reaching the whole community. They also combine an attempt to fix attention on the Bible with the attempt to reach the genuine outsider. They illustrate once again how valuable an instrument the Bible can be for making a first contact with those whom the Church does not reach.

3. *In North America*

Another type of concerted effort is that of planned Church expansion in countries that are professedly Christian. These efforts are definitely evangelistic in that they deliberately aim at reaching the outsider. The examples given are drawn from the U.S.A. in view of the fact that few countries today offer such excellent examples of planned expansion or such a wide variety of religious types. In setting out the examples, an attempt will be made to describe the methods employed and to indicate the way in which the Scriptures are used.

The first example is that of the Lutherans of the Missouri Synod, one of the most rigidly conservative churches anywhere to be found. A century ago their ancestors left Germany for North America in order to get away from what they considered to be the corroding influence of the modernism which, they felt, was eating into the life of the German Church. They paid the price of their convictions and they remain loyal to those convictions still. Although their Church is not one of the large or wealthy ones of the United States, they provide day-schools for their children without any state aid, being almost the only Protestant denomination in the U.S.A. to do this. They hold that it is worth doing, for through their schools and their churches they exercise a firm theological discipline over their people, and they claim that they lose very few of their young people through theological unsettlement or other phases of the upheavals of youth. 'We are', they say, 'well indoctrinated; we know where we stand.'

A church of this rigid theological type does not find it easy to co-operate with others and does not as a rule seek to do so. It takes little part in special evangelistic campaigns, partly because it prefers to make its own witness separately, and partly because it is not attracted to special and spasmodic efforts. As a Church they believe that evangelism should not be an occasional campaign, but a continuous activity of the Church and as normal a function as worship. The result of this steady, all-the-year-round emphasis on evangelism is seen in the fact that for the last four or five years they have been growing as rapidly as any Church in the United States.

It is at this point that their experience becomes relevant to the present enquiry, for they link this persistent evangelism with equally persistent Bible study. 'Bible study', says one of their official publications, 'is basic to all the work of the Church . . . and the Bible class is second only to the sermon.'[1] 'We are here', the same publication goes on, 'not to perpetuate the Church, but to teach the Word of God. With us it is not a case of the church service *or* the Bible class, but of the church service *and* the Bible class.'[2] They recommend every parish to have Bible classes on the same regular weekly basis as the Sunday service and to have one Bible class for every seventy-five communicants on the church-roll. They make these recommendations because it is their

[1] O. E. Feucht, *Take the Sword of the Spirit*, p. 3.   [2] *Ibid.*, p. 6.

firm conviction that the Bible is far and away the best aid
to church expansion.

The Nazarenes are about as different from the Missouri
Lutherans as two Protestant Churches could well be. Yet
they are alike in linking Bible study with evangelism. The
types of evangelism favoured by the two Churches are as
different as chalk and cheese. One is disciplined, doctrinal
and centrally controlled; the other is spontaneous, experiential
and personal.

The Church of the Nazarenes was organised in 1908
following upon a revival of the Methodist doctrine of entire
sanctification; and in less than half a century its membership
has grown to over a quarter of a million. They are not only
one of the newest but also one of the most rapidly growing
denominations in the United States. Their literature reflects
their evangelical fervour, and they probably have as large a
literary output, in proportion to their membership, as any
Church in North America. The secret of their growth, according to their own statements, is the close link that is maintained
between evangelism and the Bible. In 1948 they launched
a four-year 'Crusade for Souls', at the heart of which was
a pure flame of evangelistic passion that had its origin in
their study of the Word of God. At the end of the four
years they renewed the Crusade for another four-year period,
but with one important difference: the Bible was to be put
right in the forefront. In the first four-year period the Bible
was prominent, but not a hundred per cent. That was to be
remedied, and the Bible was to occupy the central place.
The literature now being issued in this second period deals
entirely with the Bible. Those who share in the Crusade are
being called upon to study the Bible closely, learning many
passages by heart, while the booklets which are being prepared for the workers to put into people's hands are made

up of extracts from the Bible arranged under suitable headings. They claim that they 'can already see the results. We have had one year of the second period and the new Bible-emphasis has already proved itself far more fruitful.' They hold that 'There is no better evangelist than the Scriptures' and they express their conception of the place that the Bible should have in evangelism by the slogan that they have adopted: 'To crusade for souls focus on the Bible.'

Both these Churches use the Scriptures as their main means of bringing the Gospel home to men and women. They teach their members to use the Bible in their approach to outsiders, either by reading it or by quoting it from memory. They provide their evangelistic workers with Gospel portions and with 'guides' which consist almost entirely of Bible extracts arranged with that purpose in mind. They claim that they really 'use' the Bible in their evangelistic work, and they affirm that in their experience the most permanent conversions are those that are based on the acts and promises of God as set out in the Scriptures. It is an impressive fact that these Bible-based Churches, such as the Missouri Lutherans and the Nazarenes, are everywhere increasing and form an important part of the growing edge of the Christian Church in the U.S.A. today.

A word should be added at this point lest a wrong impression should be created. It is not for one moment suggested that these are the only Churches that are carrying on active evangelistic work or winning large numbers of converts to the Christian cause. On the contrary it is gladly recognised that many of the less theologically conservative Churches are just as alive to the evangelistic need and just as eagerly winning large numbers of new members every year. Nor is it for one moment suggested that the Bible is the only tool that is or can be used. On the contrary it is, once again, fully recognised that there are other methods, such for example as visitation evangelism by lay folk that are being used with most stimulating results. Rather what is suggested is that the Bible is as a simple matter of fact being used and fruitfully used in the evangelistic activity of certain churches and groups in the U.S.A. today. Whatever may be true of other tools and other methods of evangelism, here is a tool and a method that is obviously successful, and one that is of importance for those who are concerned with the major strategy of the Christian Church.

Another sphere in which the Scriptures are proving their worth is in connection with efforts to serve the vast number of people in America who are constantly on the move. No less than twenty per cent. of the people of the U.S.A., so it is estimated, change their address every year. The majority of them tend to move westward. Some of them go from one house and town to another; others, not so fortunate, have to live under makeshift conditions, in camps or in trailer-homes. Some of them are loyal church members temporarily detached from church association, and in need of shepherding; others of them have never had any church connection, being part of the religious flotsam and jetsam of North America, and in need of evangelisation. These migrant multitudes present a problem and an opportunity of the first importance, and many of the Churches of the U.S.A., as for example the Methodists and the United Lutherans, have regarded them as a major missionary call.

Amongst the methods that the United Lutherans have adopted is the Trailer Mission which consists of a mobile Trailer Chapel and a small team of workers. A trained woman worker goes on in advance to prepare the way. She visits the trailer homes, tells the occupants about the trailer chapel that is coming and about the meetings it will provide for children, for women, and for whole families. The result is that when the chapel arrives, equipped with pastor, projector and books, it becomes at once a centre of interest. A church school for children is probably the first thing that is started; then an afternoon Bible class for women; then evening gatherings for all. Not only do the children come along with eagerness, but considerable numbers of women come in the afternoons and family groups in the evenings. The chapel stays in a camp long enough to build up a small group and to link it with the nearest existing church. By this means over 100,000 people have been brought together and formed into some 700 groups or congregations during the last eight years. This notable venture in evangelism is relevant to the present enquiry because the Bible is used in every phase of the mission's work. It is the Bible that is taught to the children in the mornings; it is the Bible that is studied by the women in the afternoons; and it is the Bible that is the centre of the meetings for adults in the evenings. Many of the children, young married couples and older folk hear the Bible and learn to read it for the first time through the agency of the trailer chapel.

In all this varied home mission work and church expansion activity of the U.S.A. the Bible has a recognised place. It is not suggested that it is the only tool that is or can be used; rather it is suggested that the Bible is in fact being used and used fruitfully in all kinds of situations. This fact no one concerned for the growth of the Christian cause can afford to neglect.

4. *In Germany*

Modern Germany presents an entirely different picture. In the U.S.A. the aim is to reach the unchurched multitudes, using the Bible as a tool. In Germany the aim is to study the Bible as the book that contains God's Word, finding in the process that this is one of the ways to the reawakening of Christian life and evangelistic activity.

For a century and more Bible classes have been a feature of Germany's religious life; but they were stereotyped and formal; and those who attended them repudiated the suggestion that they had anything to do with the problems of everyday life or with winning others to the Christian faith. Winning others, they said, was the pastor's job. After the collapse of the Nazi régime, however, a new kind of Bible class began to appear in which a deliberate attempt was made to relate Bible study to the conditions of daily living. The movement caught on, and today there are thousands of these Bible groups in Germany. The most remarkable are probably those conducted by Pastor Hamel of Halle who is said to have as many as two thousand students in his Bible groups every week. Many of them owe their origin to the Evangelical academies where groups of men and women meet on a vocational basis—all doctors, or all factory workers, or all housewives, or all engineers—for three or four days at a time. An hour is spent each morning in Bible study and the rest of the morning in hammering out the problems of the particular group. Later in the day an attempt is made to relate these problems to Christian teaching and in particular to the word of the Bible studied together in the morning. Doctors, for example, will ask what the Bible has to say about the necessity of telling a patient the whole truth about his condition, or trade unionists will ask what is the word of the Bible on fair wages or corporate bargaining. The influence of the Academies is growing, and those who attend them are encouraged to start small vocational groups on similar lines in their own towns, the meetings being generally held in private houses and led by laymen or women. These groups, in which Bible study is a feature, are one of the sources of the growth of the *Kirchentag*, which brings together thousands of layfolk every year or so from almost every part of the country. It is perhaps the most vital religious development in present-day Germany, and what is more it puts the Bible in the centre. In its great gathering in Stuttgart in 1952, for example, it was Bible study that attracted the largest attendances. In eight large tents and halls thousands of people gathered every day to study the story of Israel's exodus from Egypt, and realised, many of them for the first time, how directly the Bible speaks to man's condition. 'Is this not our situation?' they asked one another and turned again to see what else the Bible had to say to them. The new Bible groups, the Evangelical Academies and the *Kirchentag* together make up what is probably the most important renewing influence in the life of post-war Germany; and it is significant that without exception they put the Bible in the central place in their activity and draw their vitality from its pages.

One of the most obvious ways of using the Bible with evangelism as the objective is to distribute it wholesale. Ever since the Bible societies came into existence there have been people who have urged that the Bible should not be sold but given away. They have taken the view that the Book itself, like the Gospel it contains, should be a free gift and available to all. The Bible societies have never been able entirely to share this view, with the result that in more recent times organisations have come into being for the express purpose of giving rather than selling the Bible to all who are willing to receive it. In Britain the Scripture Gift Mission and the Pocket Testament League, and in the United States the Gideons, the World Gospel Crusades and the Million Testament Campaigns are amongst the best known.

The Scripture Gift Mission was founded, as its constitution says, 'to evangelise the world by the Word of God'. It distributes more than four million Gospels, New Testaments and Bibles every year, not to mention another four million texts and leaflets entirely in the words of Scripture. It distributes these through some 10,000 voluntary workers in various parts of the world, who give or sell them to individuals as they think best. The Mission does not believe in indiscriminate or broadcast distribution; it prefers careful free distribution in close association with personal evangelism. It favours the individual approach and believes that the ideal method is to give a copy of Scripture as a climax to a personal conversation. In a word, the Scripture Gift Mission regards the Bible as a means to evangelism and is ready to provide it free of charge to all who will use it for that purpose.

The Pocket Testament League had its origin in an English girls' school, when one of the pupils began to tell some of her school friends about her conversion and to try and get them to join her in carrying a pocket Testament about with them to read at odd moments and to use in talking with others. This led them to form a Pocket Testament League, and to draw up rules, viz. that those who joined were expected to read the Bible daily, to carry a New Testament with them always and to use it with a view to winning others. Years later it blossomed out as a world-wide movement. Today it gives Testaments gratis to all who promise to 'read and carry' the Bible daily, but it does not attempt widespread free distribution. Its aim is primarily evangelistic and it encourages people to read the Bible because it believes that that is the best way to win converts. In the U.S.A., however, the League has developed into an organisation for widespread free distribution. Believing that the end of the age is at hand it has felt it necessary to develop a speedier method than that in use in Great Britain, and has accordingly adopted a policy of large-scale free distribution, in combination with mass evangelism. Between 1949 and 1952 the League distributed no less than ten million Scriptures in Japan alone, using five teams of workers each equipped with a sound-unit and a truck. They preached in the open air in town and country, wherever they could get an audience, and at the end of their meetings they handed out Gospel Portions to all who were willing to receive them. Next they turned their attention to Korea, and in one year distributed half a million Gospel Portions. In 1953 they were busily distributing Scriptures in Formosa. Although the personal method of distribution seems to have been partly if not largely abandoned by the American section of the Pocket Testament League in favour of widespread free distribution, the evangelistic purpose has remained unchanged. In fact it is precisely because they regard the Bible as the most effective means of bringing the truth of God home to man's heart and mind that they give it away in such large numbers.

The Gideons, which had an almost accidental beginning through the meeting of two Christian business men in an American hotel, has from the first been a business man's organisation, aiming at winning other men to Christ, particularly by placing Bibles where they are likely to be read. In the half century of its existence, it has placed over 20,000,000 Bibles and Testaments in hotel bedrooms, doctor's waiting rooms, hospitals, prisons, camps and such-like places where people wait and are glad to have something to read. As in the other organisations concerned with widespread Scripture distribution, their aim is evangelism with the Bible as the instrument. During the last few years they have enlarged their sphere and have begun to distribute Scriptures on a large scale in Japan, Mexico and elsewhere. They have done this because of a growing sense of apocalyptic urgency and a deepening conviction that the Bible is far and away the best means of attaining the desired end. The Gideons make no attempt to compile statistics of results, being content to make the Scriptures available to those who are willing to read, in the conviction that some of the seed will fall into good soil. Occasionally, information comes through of someone who has reaped the benefit of the Gideons' action. 'During the eight months I spent on my back in bed,' writes a former hospital patient, 'my Gideons' New Testament was the best friend I had. It helped me when nothing else could. I don't know how many times I read it through.' More recently an American soldier wrote from Korea saying: 'Among my prized possessions is a Gideons' New Testament. I find that it is not only a prize, but a part of my daily life, for in it I found the way to eternal life.'

The World Gospel Crusades differs from the Gideons in that it does not itself distribute Scriptures, but makes large grants of Gospel Portions to missionaries and others who apply for them and promise to use them for definitely evangelistic purposes. They have made grants of something like two million Gospels in Formosa, three-quarters of a million in Mexico and smaller quantities in Greece, Jamaica and elsewhere. In Formosa the distribution has been part and parcel of a great evangelistic campaign, which is said to have resulted in many thousands of conversions. In Mexico Gospel Portions have been put into the hands of an enterprising young missionary who has devised a novel method of distribution which he calls 'Air Mail from God'. He packs the Gospel Portions into an aeroplane and drops them on remote villages in forest and mountain areas. His practice is to select a village and then fly 'low and slow' over it, dropping Portions in a steady stream. As he does this the villagers, old and young alike, rush out from their homes and scour the neighbourhood for the little books, and then bring them back in triumph. If he visits the village a few hours later, as he sometimes does, he finds that every copy has been carefully retrieved. Sometimes he finds a man quietly reading a copy in a shady corner, or a woman with one of the Gospels carefully tucked into her market basket, or a group of boys slowly spelling out the words one by one. He says that he has rarely if ever found a copy torn up or thrown away. What is more he has discovered that just because the books are dropped from the air the villagers are eager to possess them and they read them with an open and expectant mind. How long it will take for the novelty to wear off no one can say, but in the meantime the method is not only enterprising, it is fruitful. It is worth adding that the missionary in question has now developed a method of follow-up which is already proving a valuable means of conserving the results.

Of these various organisations that practise free and widespread Scripture distribution, two recommend that the Scriptures should be given individually and as the climax of a conversation. They maintain that this personal and individual method is the most fruitful from the evangelistic point of view. The others, believing that Christ's Second Coming is imminent, feel it necessary to adopt more speedy and wholesale methods. They believe that by these methods the largest possible number of people will have the chance of learning something of the Gospel while there is yet time. But whether the method of distribution is individual or whether it is wholesale, is not relevant to the present enquiry. What is relevant is that in all cases the Scriptures are used as a means of winning men and women to Christ.

The same may be said about a somewhat similar issue, namely whether the Scriptures should be sold or given away. Selling them is said to have more fruitful results, while giving

them gratis is said to reach a larger number. A whole array
of arguments can be produced on either side. But whether
the Scriptures are sold or whether they are given matters
little to the present enquiry. What matters is the fact that
those who favour selling and those who believe in giving
gratis agree in regarding the Bible as a prime means of
evangelisation.

5. *Audio-Visual Aids*

Some of the most remarkable developments in recent years
in bringing the gospel to the attention of large numbers of
people have been through the use of audio-visual aids, such
as the radio, the cinema, the drama and the newspaper. In
all these forms of extensive evangelism, the Bible has played
a significant part.

In radio the religious developments of recent years have
been far greater than is generally realised. There are now
several Christian radio stations, the best known of which is
'The Voice of the Andes'. This is the pioneer missionary
broadcasting station, and for over twenty years it has been
broadcasting the gospel from its headquarters at Quito in
Ecuador. Its broadcasts have been mainly in Spanish, Portu-
guese and English, but it has recently been sending out over
one thousand programmes a month in eleven different languages. Not content with that, it is now raising its power and
range to the point where its voice will penetrate all 'curtains'
and encircle the entire globe. Other Christian radio stations
have been set up in the Philippines, known as 'The Call of
the Orient', in Costa Rica, called 'The Voice of the Carib-
bean' and at other strategic points around the world. In addition to these specifically Christian radio stations, broadcasting
networks and corporations in many countries include Christian broadcasts in their regular programmes. In Scotland in

1950 the broadcasting corporation went so far as to conduct a radio mission, and to do it again in 1952, in happy co-operation with the evangelistic programme of the Scottish churches. It is no exaggeration to say that by means of the radio the Christian gospel is heard in millions of homes and in every part of the world. Radio has probably done more than any other single agency in modern times to extend the range of Christian evangelism.

It must not, however, be thought that it is only the Christian message that is broadcast; it is also the authentic words of Scripture. The Bible itself is read, and often very well read, and its words frequently make a deep impression. Nor is that all. The radio helps not only to familiarise listeners with the actual words of the Bible, but also to circulate the book itself. In Japan, for example, one missionary society has been receiving fifteen hundred requests for Scriptures every month through their radio work. 'The Voice of the Andes' after a month of readings from St. Luke had so many requests for copies of the Gospel that its stock was completely exhausted. In Brazil thousands of Scriptures are asked for every year by radio listeners. The Brazil Baptists make a practice in their weekly broadcasts of offering to send a Gospel to any listeners who apply. They get something like twenty thousand requests a year. Their practice is that when they send the Gospel they invite the reader, when he has read it, to write for a New Testament, and when he has read that, to apply for a Bible. Continuous reading is thus encouraged, and in hundreds of known cases it has led on step by step to profession of faith and full church membership.

In addition to this, another development of great importance for the present enquiry has been taking place in recent years. Bible courses have been organised on the air. One radio station has a Bible study course that runs for twenty-four consecutive weeks. Another has a short course that goes out in several languages. Yet another has frequent short courses for schools. The National Council of the Churches of Christ in the U.S.A. has recently made an enquiry into the attempt to associate Bible study with evangelism over the air, and has expressed its genuine satisfaction. It seems beyond question that in radio as in other means of communicating the Gospel, the Bible can play an important part.

In the cinema world the situation is somewhat different. There are specifically Christian organisations producing and distributing films which aim at advancing the Christian cause, and there are also commercial concerns that are willing to produce and to exhibit films that have a clear Christian message. Organisations like Religious Films Ltd. in Britain, or like Cathedral Films in the United States, are actively engaged in producing and distributing films that have a definite Christian purpose. Some of them have been at work for several years and not without a measure of success, though the scale of their work is completely dwarfed by the gigantic operations of the cinema world. In addition to these definitely Christian organisations, there are some cinema corporations that are willing to exhibit films with a Christian purpose, provided they come up to all the usual standards. There have been many notable examples of such films.

It is abundantly clear that the cinema can be a powerful evangelistic agency; what is not so clear is what part the Bible can play. There are, of course, films that feature the Bible, showing how it is produced and distributed and used in various parts of the world. But they are mainly for the information of people already interested. They are part of the educational and propaganda material used by Bible societies amongst Christian people. The urgent need is for something more and something different, namely for Bible films

that are definitely intended to be shown to people who make
no Christian profession. Very little thought has been given
to this aspect of the subject, and the time has come for it to
be actively investigated.

Drama has always offered great religious opportunities,
and at times has been closely associated with the Christian
Church. For long periods it was one of the Church's most
valuable evangelistic agencies. The miracle and morality plays
that were for centuries a feature of Europe's life were means
not only of edifying the faithful, but also of influencing the
non-Christian. 'The Passion Play of Oberammergau' is a
notable example that has survived into modern times. Deliberate attempts have been made in recent years to revive the
drama as an agency for spreading the faith. One of the best-
known in English is Dorothy Sayers' *The Man Born to be
King*, which not only deals with a Bible theme but does it,
as far as possible, in Bible language. Ventures of a somewhat
similar kind have been undertaken in Germany, Holland,
France, Sweden and elsewhere, while in India and to a less
extent in China, the old-time indigenous drama has been
revived in the interest of Christian evangelism.

The Christian *Kalakshepam* in India has proved a most
fruitful method of communicating the gospel message to
the masses of the people. In essence it consists of an alterna-
tion of speech and song built up round some Bible episode.
The story-teller recounts the episode in vivid detail, using,
as far as possible, the language of the vernacular Bible. After
a few minutes of speaking, the story-teller and his friends
burst into song, singing to some old Indian melody a Christian lyric or hymn that suits the theme. This finished, the
story-teller takes up his tale again and once more, after a few
minutes of speech, there is another burst of song. In this
fashion they go on for hour after hour, alternating story and

song, until listeners have not only caught the lilt and words of the song but have also become familiar with at least one biblical episode or theme. The method has already proved its evangelistic value, especially amongst village folk, while its dependence on the Bible is obvious.

In all these new ventures in the realms of radio, cinema and drama, there are great evangelistic possibilities, and in all of them the actual words of the Bible can be, and sometimes are, used with great effect. But in these media, the Bible itself, as a tangible object, does not pass from one person to another, and in the nature of the case there can only occasionally be any personal contact or subsequent follow-up.

Other forms of extensive evangelism in which the Bible plays a part are such enterprises as Newspaper Evangelism, Postal Evangelism, Leaflet Evangelism, etc. These enterprises consist in inserting brief articles or advertisements or Bible passages in newspapers or mail orders, and inviting enquiries.

Newspaper Evangelism has met with particular success in Japan. It is a method that is specially suited to a highly literate country where so many people read newspapers. One advertisement recently inserted by the National Christian Council produced nearly two thousand enquiries. To a less extent the method has been used in other non-Christian lands. It has, for example, been successfully used in Madras where newspapers are fairly widely read. In the nature of the case it is difficult to assess the value of the method. Many of those who make enquiries lose interest and fade out. Others persist and in time become Christians. Such evidence as is available seems to show that from the point of view of evangelism this is not a method to be despised, while from the point of view of the Bible cause, it is to be encouraged for it is largely based on the reading and study of the Scriptures.[1]

[1] Murray Walton, *Newspaper Evangelism in Japan*, p. 89.

An interesting venture now attracting a good deal of attention in many countries is that of Bible Correspondence Courses. In India it had its origin in newspaper evangelism. Paragraphs or advertisements were inserted in papers like *The Hindu* of Madras and *The Hindustan Times* of Delhi, putting questions about religion and making brief statements about Christianity. Readers who were interested were invited to join a Bible Correspondence Course. An Easter advertisement in *The Hindustan Times* brought in over one hundred requests to join a course. A series of meetings in Vellore conducted by Dr. Stanley Jones brought in 450 requests. The movement has gone on gathering strength and is now being conducted in nine languages in India and Ceylon. Bishop Newbigin of the Church of South India says that he knows of several Bible Correspondence Courses, one of them with 12,000 members. The courses are carefully planned and often take several months to complete. If a student is merely curious he probably does not complete the course, but if he goes right through with it a permanent impression is almost certainly made upon his life. One such student recently wrote, 'I was a Hindu, but now I believe in Jesus Christ and have been baptised'. Another, a high-school boy, wrote asking for more books and saying that he would like a personal interview after his examinations were over. The courses are entirely biblical and are evidently an important means of bringing the Gospel to people's attention.

Bible Correspondence Courses have also caught on in other Asian countries, particularly amongst prisoners of war in Southern Korea and Chinese troops in Formosa. In 1951 thousands of prisoners in Korea enrolled and over 2,000 of them completed the course. In Formosa in the next year over 50,000 soldiers in Chiang Kai Shek's army enrolled as students, and something like 3,000 completed the course. So far the result has been that large numbers of Gospels have been circulated, many have been studied, and in some cases conversions have taken place.

An important new field for evangelism has been opened up in recent years through the exciting developments in the fight with illiteracy. Largely through the pioneer work of Dr. Frank Laubach, a missionary in the Philippines, a technique has been worked out whereby illiterates can be taught to read in an incredibly short time. Not only missions but governments in many parts of the world have become interested and have invited Dr. Laubach to carry out experiments in their areas. The success has been so marked that it is now estimated that many millions of people are learning to read every year. In the first instance, Dr. Laubach launched his drive against illiteracy as a venture, not in education, but in evangelism. Illiteracy was the chief obstacle in the path of his work as a missionary, and he set himself to wrestle with it in order that the Gospel might have free course. The charts and texts that he prepared were related to the Bible and aimed at enabling a man to read the New Testament as a step towards becoming a Christian. Those charts and texts—which, with some adaptation, are now being used in many parts of the world—were so planned that, in the very act of learning to read, the beginner was becoming familiar with the words of the Bible itself. Similarly, as he made progress in his reading, he was becoming more and more familiar with the biblical message. The millions of new literates have thus got their feet on the path that may later lead to full acceptance of the Christian faith. The Bible has helped to get them to that stage, and Bible Portions, prepared with care and understanding, may play an important part in helping them still further along the path.

It is at this point that urgency arises. Those millions of

new literates constitute what is probably the greatest evangelistic opportunity of today. They have a new skill and are eager to develop it. If at this psychological moment the Bible, in some suitable part or form, is put into their hands, there may result one of the greatest accessions to the Christian Church in modern times.

This survey of the way in which the Scriptures are used in concerted evangelistic efforts has pointed directly to certain conclusions. The first is that in all the varied types of present-day evangelism, whether in Brazil or India, Costa Rica or Thailand, the Bible is an important, and some would say an indispensable, instrument. The second is that this is true not only in the 'mission field' but also in many so-called Christian countries. For example, in the multifarious home-mission and church-extension activities of the U.S.A. today, or at least in the work of the denominations that are said to be growing most rapidly, the Bible is a central and an essential element. The third is that in the evangelistic activities carried on in many lands through the radio, the cinema and the newspaper, the Bible is playing an increasingly important part. The inference seems to be beyond question that the Bible has a place of such importance today in concerted evangelistic efforts that those concerned for the welfare of the world-wide Christian cause cannot fail to give it their serious attention.

Part Three

CONCLUSIONS

IN THIS THIRD and final part an attempt will be made to draw out the significance of the foregoing chapters for the Christian cause as a whole, and for the organised churches in particular. As a result of developments in theological thinking and of the circumstances of the time, the Bible cause has been invested with a new urgency. It is recognised that the King's business requires haste. The evangelisation of the world in this generation, which was the professed aim of Christian youth half a century ago, was not as foolish as many people were inclined to think. If the aim had been achieved, the whole course of recent history might have been very different. In any case it is clear to everyone now that the Christian's fight is with 'principalities and powers and spiritual wickedness in high places', that is with the world heresies, false doctrines, vicious propaganda, and conditioned thinking of our time. The tyranny of today is spiritual and psychological even more than economic and political. It is of the kind that cannot be destroyed by larger and more devilish weapons, but by stronger and more Christian ideas. This struggle is not something to be fought in the future; it is being fought today.

The foregoing chapters have also shown that the weapon that is more needed than any other is at hand; it is at hand in great quantities, and in all the main languages of the world. It is behind all curtains, iron or bamboo. It is read openly or in secret in every country on earth. It has proved its ability to speak to men of every condition, country and culture. It is the weapon *par excellence* of the Church's warfare which, if well wielded, may have a large part in winning the world for Christ. It is the Bible.

VII

FINDINGS OF THE ENQUIRY

1. *The Bible has always been used in Evangelism*

THE association between the Bible and evangelism is as old as the Bible itself. The earliest examples of Christian preaching are hardly more than quotations of Scripture strung together. At first it was the Old Testament that was quoted, as that was, right at the beginning, the only acknowledged Scripture the Church possessed. But before long quotations from the new writings crept in and became increasingly frequent. But whether the quotations were from the Old Testament or the New, the important thing is that they were used in addressing non-Christians. They were evidently regarded as a suitable means of presenting the Christian message to those outside the Church's life and of winning converts to the faith. The Scriptures continued to be used in this fashion right through the period of the Early Church, and indeed right on until the Bible began to pass out of the hands of the laity into those of the clergy. Just in proportion as the Bible ceased to be used as a layman's book, so it ceased to be used as an instrument of evangelism. It was the Reformers who rescued it from neglect, and not only gave it a central place in the Church's life, but also brought it back again into the hands of the people. With occasional aberrations that centrality has been maintained, and in the centuries since the Reformation the Bible has played a vitalising part, especially in the great renewal eras of the Church's life. One of those periods was, of course, the Reformation itself, others were the Puritan and Pietist movements, the Evangelical

Revival and the modern missionary enterprise. In all these creative eras the Bible fulfilled a double function. On the one hand it prepared the way for the new flowering of Christian life, for in each case a renewal of interest in the Bible was a prelude to the new outburst of Christian ardour and advance. On the other hand, it was the spearpoint of the new movements as they pushed ahead, for in each case the Bible was the weapon that they used. It first prepared the way and then led the advance.

Whether it was the whole Bible or only a part that was used seems to have been a matter of expediency. There was certainly never any strict requirement that the whole Bible must be used. Nor indeed could there be. In many cases only parts of the Bible had been translated. Also, in pre-printing days, the entire Bible was so expensive and so unwieldy that few people possessed one. The position was very similar to that in many parts of the mission field today. In only a small proportion of the languages spoken nowadays does the whole Bible exist; and where it does exist only a proportion of the members of the churches can afford to buy one; they have to be content with a part. The result is that it is Portions and New Testaments that are mostly used in the actual work of evangelism. Nearly ten times as many Portions and Testaments as compared with complete Bibles are circulated every year in the world as a whole. The Portion or Testament is the book with which, for the most part, the first contact with the non-Christian is made. It is thus pre-eminently the evangelist's book. Only at a later stage is the whole Bible found to be fully suitable. That was the reason why leaders of the Early Church, like Gregory of Nazianzus and Cyprian, advocated the use of certain parts of the Bible for young people and for new converts. But whether it was the whole Bible or only a part, the significance for today is that the

Scriptures in some shape or form have always been used in the Church's evangelistic work.

2. *The Bible is the best Evangelistic tool there is*

A second inference from the foregoing chapters is that most people who are actively engaged in extensive or intensive evangelism agree that the Bible is an important factor in their work. Some would go further and say that it is the most important factor of all and that there is no other worth considering. The evidence that has been given has certainly demonstrated pretty clearly that in all forms of evangelism, whether at home or abroad, the Bible has a place of front-rank importance and one that is not shared with any other agency.

'We should be completely lost without the Scriptures', says an American missionary in Pakistan. 'They are the spearhead of our evangelism. We go into the bazaars and *melas* carrying Scriptures in our hands, and we lift them up saying: "Here are books." That starts the conversation.' A British missionary in Northern Rhodesia, writing about his African evangelists, says: 'If they had not got the Bible, they could not carry on. Year in and year out it is their regular evangelistic tool. They rely on it in all their teaching and preaching.' Others express themselves a little less emphatically perhaps, but with an equally strong conviction that the Bible is without rival as an agent of evangelism. A well-known Christian leader in Belgium writes, 'The best evangelistic work is done when the Bible is in the forefront. Here in Belgium evangelism goes ahead when the Bible is well distributed and well used.' A leading evangelist in Ceylon, speaking about his own evangelistic work, says, 'I regard the Bible as an almost indispensable tool'. A missionary in India, with considerable experience of evangelism, takes a similar view, saying, 'The Bible is our main evangelistic instrument. We should never think of going out into the villages without it.' In Korea when it was decided to launch an evangelistic campaign aiming at a million converts, an immediate order was placed for a million copies of St. Mark's Gospel. In Madagascar, according to a well-informed missionary, 'the churches grew after the persecution period so long as the Bible classes continued; they wilted when the classes fell off'. Similarly, a missionary looking back on pre-Communist China said that 'those churches grew that used the Bible regularly, the others made little progress'. Add to that the evidence of those who work amongst Chicago's derelicts, or among America's migrants, or in Billy Graham's enquiry rooms. Add yet again the fact that many of the most vigorous churches of Latin America trace their origin to the visit of some colporteur who came to their neighbourhood with only a Bible in his hand, and that many of the most rapidly-growing denominations of the United States are precisely those that make the fullest use of the Bible as an instrument of evangelism.

Experience in all parts of the world and in all types of evangelism seems to point to the conclusion that the Bible is the most valuable evangelistic tool that has yet been found. It is not claimed that it is the only tool. A missionary of wide experience in Africa says quite frankly that 'the Bible is not the only operative factor in evangelism, though it may be the chief one. There are other tools for the evangelist to use, such as hymns, pictures or dramatic representations.' There most certainly are other means, but they have only a limited scope and usefulness. They are suitable for this or that particular type of situation or for this or that particular time. The Bible, however, is under no such limitations. It is the only evangelistic agency that has been used always and everywhere with success.

3. The Bible gives the Cutting Edge

If the foregoing chapters have shown anything, they have shown that the Bible is an invaluable aid in evangelism of all kinds, in all countries, and at all periods. So far as evangelism is concerned, the Bible plays a unique part. 'Jesus, God, I do believe', cried a Mongolian pilgrim to Tibet as he read and re-read the copy of St. Mark that had been put into his hands.[1] 'A little company of believers', writes a colporteur in Brazil, 'has been established here in São João around a copy of the Scriptures.'[2] The Bible confronts men with Christ and brings them to a decision.

This is all the more remarkable when it is recalled that Jesus Himself neither wrote a book nor encouraged His disciples to do so. Nor did He at any time indicate that a book would play a vital part in the spreading of the Gospel. By some strange virtue of its own, the Bible has won its special place as the best agent of evangelism anywhere to be found. And in saying this the reference is not merely to the message of the Bible, but also to the physical book itself as the bearer of the message. The very concreteness of the Bible, as something that can be seen and handled, has not been a hindrance but a help. It has been a constant corrective of that kind of subjective interpretation that is based on the theological views or personal idiosyncrasies of the individual. It has also brought evangelism down to earth. The continual temptation in evangelistic work is to be content with public exhortation or private conversation, that is to say, with words. The Bible's tangible reality has the effect of making the talking take shape and form as when 'the Word became flesh and dwelt amongst us'.

A second fact that has emerged from the foregoing chapters

[1] W. H. Hudspeth, *The Bible and China*, p. 39.
[2] *American Bible Society Report*, *1937*, p. 175.

LBWB

is that, as far as evangelism is concerned, the place of the Bible is in the front line. It is above everything else the tool of the pioneer. It is what practically every evangelist takes with him when he sets out to contact non-Christians, and what practically every church worker is supplied with when he starts on a house-to-house visitation campaign. It is the best contact-maker as every colporteur knows. It is also the best conscience-prober as countless converts can attest. In a wide variety of circumstances and cultures men have read the Bible, with a minimum of exegetical help, yet through it have found the word of life. Bishop Pickett, in his classic study of *Mass Movements in India*, shows that again and again it was a Gospel Portion that brought a flash of light to a man's heart and sent him, Gospel in hand, to tell his family and relatives, and so set going what grew to be a mass or community movement. Bishop Berggrav relates that as a schoolboy he was ashamed to have it known that he was the son of a pastor. But one day he was challenged by another boy for his attitude and told that he should read the Bible, beginning with the Epistle to the Romans. Young Berggrav followed the advice and started in on 'Romans'. When, however, he came to the phrase 'I am not ashamed of the gospel of Christ', his conscience was stirred to such effect that the Apostle's words became the turning point of his life. In countless cases the Bible has been the means, and often the only means, as far as one can see, that God has used to win individuals or whole groups to Himself. 'We record the conviction', wrote the Commission sent to Korea some years ago by the American Presbyterian Mission, 'that the unique and dominant place given to instruction in the Scriptures has been the outstanding factor through these fifty years in the evangelisation of Korea. . . . The very large development of the system of Bible classes and conferences and the short-term Bible institutes in every station, have been a prime factor in the conservation of the Church and its extension.'[1]

No one can delve into the records of Bible societies, colportage associations, evangelisation crusades and similar bodies, without being brought face to face with the fact that it is the Bible, more than anything else, that brings a man to decision. What conversation often fails to do, what preaching does not accomplish, what friendly counselling does not succeed in doing, the Bible seems able to achieve. Merely to say that the Bible plays an important part in evangelism is clearly not enough. Something more positive and specific is needed by way of explanation. The simple fact is that the Bible seems to supply something that is missing in many forms of evangelism. It supplies something that pierces through a man's defences and gets right home, something that is 'quick and powerful, and sharper than any two-edged sword'. The Bible, in a word, provides evangelism with its cutting edge.

4. *The Bible is for Everyman*

According to their own statement, the Scriptures were written in order that men might believe that Jesus is the Christ, and that believing they might have life in His name. Their purpose was quite frankly evangelistic. Their place, therefore, is not in the archives of the Church, but in the hands and homes of the people. The Bible is meant for everyman. And the periods when the Church has been most active in getting it to everyman have been precisely the periods when the Church has grown most rapidly. For the Church's own sake, as well as for the sake of the Kingdom, Bible distribution ought to be a regular part of the Church's

[1] T. S. Soltau, *Korea: Hermit Nation and its Response to Christianity*, p. 120.

task. The annual circulation has been growing steadily year by year and now runs into millions. The present-day figures are truly staggering. They show an average circulation over the last half a dozen years of more than 20 million Scriptures a year.

To publish and circulate over 20 million Bibles, Testaments and Portions in a year is a stupendous achievement, and one that has no parallel in the realm of books. It is even more stupendous in its consequences, for who can say what the effect of these millions of Scriptures is in lives changed and churches planted? There is no means of measuring how great this contribution is. All that one can say is that it is a major contribution towards the conversion of the world, and that without it the Christian cause would be in a sorry plight.

But however impressive the figures may be, it is well to bear in mind that at the present rate it will take one hundred years to put a copy of the Scriptures into the hands of every human being! On the score of the figures, therefore, there is little ground for complacency.

There is still less ground for complacency from another point of view. According to the statistics published by the French Academy, there are 2,378 languages spoken in the world today. Of these only 190 have the complete Bible and another 937 have some part of it. Fully half the languages of the world do not possess so much as a single sentence of Scripture. Obviously there is still plenty of translation work to be done. And plenty of distribution work too. For with 1,000 million people at present able to read and an additional 50 million each year learning to read, how is it possible to catch up, much less to keep pace with the need? The answer depends to a large extent on the seriousness with which the Church as a whole recognises its obligation and responds to it.

5. *The Bible is being fruitfully used in Evangelism*

Far and away the most fruitful method of Scripture distribution is that of colportage, remembering, of course, that colporteurs may be full-time or part-time, paid or unpaid. The practice of distributing the Bible personally and one by one has been seen to be fully justified. By this method there is a personal encounter, a conversation, a testimony, a recommendation. This method is probably sound from the point of view of salesmanship; it is unquestionably sound from the point of view of evangelism. It provides a personal contact, and in evangelistic work it is personal contact that counts.

Fifty years ago there were paid colporteurs in almost every country in which it was possible for the Bible to circulate. But during the last half-century colportage has tended to fall into abeyance, at any rate in certain countries, and there are by no means as many full-time colporteurs at work today as there were fifty years ago. But if the number of full-time paid colporteurs has fallen off, the number of part-time, voluntary distributors has vastly increased. Not only are there more Scriptures being sold today than ever before, but also there are more men and women selling them. Counting all these helpers as colporteurs, for that in fact is what they are, it is true to say that the most fruitful method of distributing the Bible, as judged by the evangelistic results, is that of colportage—the personal, individual method in which every book sold means that a contact has been made and a word of commendation spoken, or a Christian testimony given.

The second method which the enquiry shows to have been fruitful is that of united efforts in which all the Christian forces in a city or district combine to organise Weeks of Witness, Bible campaigns, Bible weeks or months, and similar ventures. They aim at getting every church member to take his part in distributing the Scriptures and witnessing to his faith.

This not only makes an impression on those who take part, but also on their neighbours and the whole community. The method calls for thorough preparation, for a combination of house-to-house visitation with public gatherings, and, not least, for careful follow-up. Where these features are observed the results in Bible sales and Christian impact are impressive and often lasting.

The third method of using the Bible with a view to evangelism is that of widespread free distribution. The method is particularly popular in the United States where it receives generous support. That it yields fruit in changed lives is fairly certain, though by the very nature of the case it is difficult to produce much evidence and in any case most of the organisations concerned make no attempt to do so. They do not, generally speaking, advocate indiscriminate distribution to all and sundry, for they know that from the point of view of evangelism personal and individual distribution bears the best fruit. But they realise that there are countless multitudes of human beings who have never seen the Bible or heard its message, and believing that the time is short they have devised ways of speeding up the process of Bible distribution.

A fourth method that the enquiry has revealed as having considerable possibilities is the use of the radio, the cinema, the drama and the press as means of bringing the Word of God to multitudes of people at present unreached. These media have now been sufficiently utilised to make some appraisal of their value possible. In all of them it is the message and words of the Bible rather than the Bible itself that is in the focus of attention. In some of them it is possible to organise Bible study, but in general these new facilities and techniques do not bring people into living contact with one another, nor do they confront people with the Bible so much as with the truths which the Bible contains. Considerable attention, however, is being given to these problems, and progress can be expected in due time. Already it is possible to organise Sunday schools and Bible Correspondence Classes by means of the radio. Already the cinema, the drama and the press have shown how they can play their part in making themselves serviceable in the cause of evangelism.

As this enquiry clearly shows, there are good and bad ways of using these four methods, the need being to show which are the good and fruitful ones. It happens, however, that in spite of the many studies of evangelism in recent years very little attention has been given to the use of the Bible in evangelism. There are hardly any appraisals of experiments, much less manuals of guidance. It is a comparatively neglected field. If this enquiry has shown anything, it has shown that the Scriptures can be used with very fruitful results. What is needed now is that studies should be initiated and experiments collated. For this purpose nothing would be better than that some central body of the Churches should stimulate studies and experiments and gather up the results for the guidance of all the churches everywhere.

6. *The Challenge is now to the Churches and their Leaders*

What is the significance of this enquiry and its importance for the Church as a whole, in particular for those who are entrusted with the responsibility of leadership?

That the Bible has something of importance to contribute to the Church's evangelistic task is the central contention of this book. It has been used always and everywhere in evangelism. Where it has been neglected, interest in evangelism has tended to flag. When it has been keenly used and eagerly distributed evangelism has prospered. More than that, it has secured results that no other Christian agency has been able

to achieve. It has shown itself possessed of a power to influence individuals and even communities, bringing them
somehow into the very presence of the living God. It has, of
course, been abused and made an instrument of division and
distress; but it has also, and far more often, been the means
in God's hands, of bringing blessing and enrichment. It has
brought some of the world's most abandoned men to a
completely new way of life; it has been the means of calling
into being new worshipping communities; and it has been
at the source of many of the great renewal movements in the
life of the Church from the days of the Apostles onwards.
'Nearly all the renewals and moral reforms within Christianity have sprung', writes F. R. Barry, 'from the rediscovery
of Scripture, and especially the Synoptic Gospels. The
moment Christianity loses touch with the inspiration of the
New Testament it tends to sink to a sub-Christian level, and
its moral witness is weakened or obscured.'[1]

The inference is obvious. For its own sake as well as for
that of the Kingdom, the Church must make a greater use of
this instrument that lies half neglected in its hands. It must
no longer be content to render lip-service; it must take a full
share in the work of distribution. It must set before its
members the ideal of every Christian sharing in this service
and must enrol them literally by tens of thousands for the work
of evangelism through Scripture distribution. The churches
should regard Bible distribution as part and parcel of their
evangelistic task. The Bible societies by themselves cannot be
expected to translate and print the Scriptures in all the
languages of the world and in addition to distribute the tens
of millions of Scriptures that are needed every year. The
triple task of translation (including revision), production and
distribution is beyond the capacity of a score or so of

[1] F. R. Barry, *The Relevance of Christianity*, p. 40.

voluntary organisations. It must be shared by the whole Church and not left to an enthusiastic and devoted few.

There is no suggestion that the churches do not at present take any share in distributing the Scriptures. They do. Some of them take a very large share; but others scarcely do a hand's turn. What is suggested is that the time has come for the churches as a whole to regard Scripture distribution as an important part of their responsibility.

The present enquiry has shown that the man who passes on the Scriptures is sharing in the Church's front-line work. Scripture distribution, especially where it is accompanied by a personal testimony, may be as truly a part of the work of the Church as preaching a sermon or serving on a foreign missions committee. The time has come to put it on a recognised footing as an honoured form of Christian service.

And not only honoured but fruitful. Bible distribution achieves results. As in every other form of seed-sowing, there are disappointments, some of the seed falling by the wayside, or on stony ground. But this enquiry has shown that by and large steady Bible distribution means steady Christian expansion.

And not only fruitful but timely. A new wave of interest in the Bible is a mark of present-day religious life. The Bible is coming back into the centre in theology and in preaching. Those who come into Bible work now come in on a flowing tide.

The world's growing population and the addition of millions of new literates every year is raising the demand for books to proportions never known before. The Bible is sure to be called for in great and growing numbers. Also if the rising standards of education and literary taste are to be heeded, and especially if evangelism is to get home to the common man, there will have to be a great deal of revision of existing versions in the years ahead. With translation, revision and production the Bible societies will have plenty to do. They will, in the first place, have to translate, revise and print the Scriptures. They will in the second place have to retain responsibility for circulating the Scriptures in the areas where the Church does not yet exist, or where it is weak and immature, or where it is overshadowed by an unfriendly government or dominant religion. They will in the third place have to go on making grants to the indigenous churches to help them in their distribution work. This broad division of function should of course be flexibly applied as differing situations require. The churches must recognise that Bible distribution is their task and should gradually take it over. The Bible societies must retain responsibility for the translation, revision and production of the Scriptures, for distribution in areas where the Church is non-existent or still very young, and for giving grants where they are required. This will enable the Bible societies to focus all their energies upon their particular and technical tasks, and will also call out from the churches new resources of initiative and service, which in turn will stimulate and enrich its life.

The Bible is an unrivalled instrument of evangelism. What is more it is probably better able to play a decisive part in the Christian movement today than at any time in living memory. For it holds a unique position. It can penetrate where no missionary can go; it can speak when other voices are silenced; and it can remain when Christian workers are removed from the scene. It is capable of being more than ever before the means whereby men of every nation and kindred and tongue can hear the wonderful works of God. It is for the churches to make full use of it.

GENERAL INDEX